A Western Horseman Book

Colorado Springs,

REINING

By Al Dunning

with Pat Close

Photographs by Kurt Markus

REINING

Published by
Western Horseman Inc.

3850 North Nevada Ave.
Box 7980
Colorado Springs, CO 80933-7980

Design, Typography, and Production
Western Horseman
Colorado Springs, Colorado

Printing
McCormick-Armstrong Co., Inc.
Colorado Springs, Colorado

Tenth Printing: November 1994

ISBN 0-911647-02-3

D E D I C A T I O N

This book is dedicated to those unique individuals who
have entered into the vocation of horse training not solely
to achieve monetary rewards, but to enjoy and appreciate
the athletic abilities and individual personalities of horses,
to respect the outdoor life, and to use their special talents to
enrich the lives of others through horses.

AL DUNNING

CONTENTS

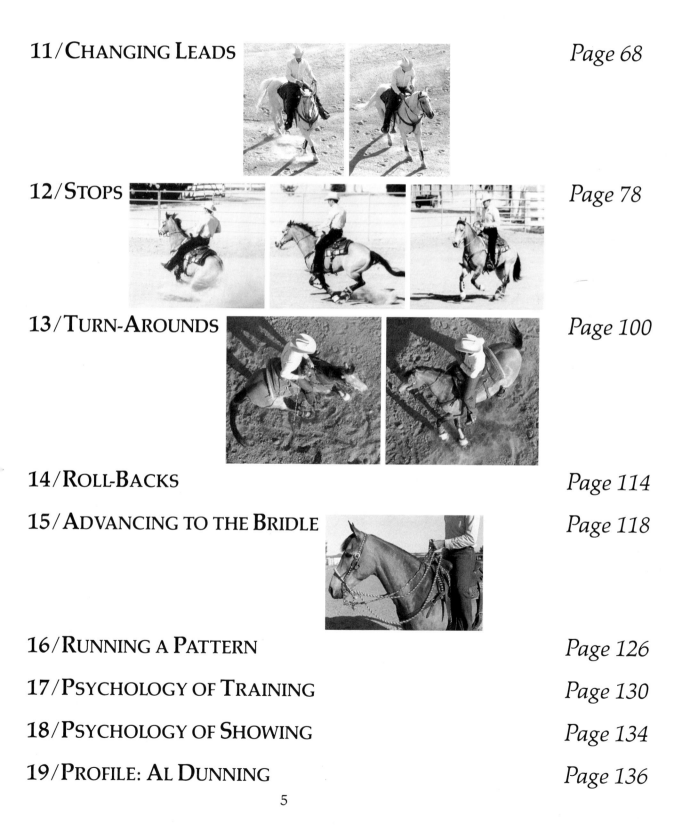

INTRODUCTION

Today's reining horse has evolved from the cowboy's everyday ranch work of efficiently maneuvering cattle on the open range. When moving, holding, and sorting cattle, a cowboy needs an agile saddle horse that is quick on his feet, can be controlled by a light rein, and has an explosive start and stop.

In years gone by, cowboys and vaqueros prided themselves on riding these hard-working horses and enjoyed challenging one another to see whose mount could stop harder, slide farther, and turn around faster. It was the beginning of the reining horse competition we know today.

Reining developed on the West Coast, but has gradually spread eastward, and in recent years its popularity has soared. As a spectator event, it ranks as one of the most popular in the equine world, and the excitement it generates is assurance that reining will have a strong role in future equine competition.

Almost every major breed association offers reining classes, or stock horse classes, as they are also known. One of the first associations to sanction them was the American Horse Shows Association, which for years has offered year-end high-point awards in national and regional stock horse competition.

Adjusting some equipment during an early morning ride in the desert.

Many of our good reining horses are also shown in cowhorse classes.

Today, the organization that gets the lion's share of credit for popularizing the event in the Midwest and East is the National Reining Horse Association. Through NRHA leadership, reining horses have become an industry that offers substantial financial rewards—not only in purse money, but also in the breeding, raising, and training of these athletic horses.

Yet, it's still relatively easy for a newcomer or beginner to break into reining horse competition; and one does not necessarily have to spend megabucks for a good prospect, as in some other equine events. A good one just might come sliding in from anywhere.

The future of reining horses has never looked brighter. The NRHA is growing, with an ever-increasing number of affiliate chapters in various states. And thanks to the NRHA and AQHA non-pro events, more amateurs are getting involved. They are finding that reining offers a challenge, and that it's an incomparable thrill to be astride a powerful horse who can turn around so fast everything blurs, then run down the arena at top speed to lock down and slide 20 or 30 feet.

Reining is a great sport, with its roots straight from the American West. It has been extremely rewarding to my family and myself, and it is with pleasure that I share with you through this book some of my ideas on training the reining horse. I hope that the book will be helpful to every reader, rider, and spectator.

—Al Dunning

Cherizan, an outstanding all-around mare, is now one of our broodmares. My wife Becky rode Cherizan to win the 1969 Arizona Quarter Horse Breeders Assn. youth all-around award.
LeRoy Weathers Photo

1 SELECTING THE HORSE

"It's better—and a lot easier—to start with the right kind of breeding, then look for the right kind of conformation."

When I'm looking for a young reining prospect, the first thing I consider is breeding. It's just like shopping for a race horse at the yearling sales; ideally, you want a colt or filly by a sire that has proven himself, and out of a mare that either won, or has produced foals that have won.

I like a reining horse prospect to be by a stallion that showed he can get down on his hocks and use himself; and I would prefer him to be out of a mare that is a known producer...more so than a mare who was a winner, but hasn't produced anything. Many mares who win a bunch in the show ring or on the track never produce anything good. If you buy a colt out of a mare that has already foaled a winning reining horse, you have a better chance of getting a good one, even if he's by a different sire than his half-brother or sister.

As far as particular bloodlines, there are many today capable of turning out good reining horses. I feel that as long as you stick with proven bloodlines, and don't get too contemporary, you'll do okay. A horse can be contemporary on one side, but he better have some foundation breeding on the other side or he might not turn out as good as you'd like.

By contemporary, I mean Doc Bar or Thoroughbred breeding, and by foundation, King or Leo. I really like King-bred mares; they're my favorites because you can cross them on so many different bloodlines and get good colts. They won't all be good, of course, but that kind of breeding cuts down your risk.

Because there are so many different breeding possibilities, I personally don't want to own a stud, at least not right now, because I like to breed my mares to different stallions. It's like Hank Wies-

camp once said, "If a mare has a good foal by one stud, there's no reason why she might not have a better one by another stud." If you have your own stud, you're locked into breeding to him.

Sometimes you'll stumble onto a good reining horse that wasn't bred to be one, but just happened to be born with the right kind of conformation, ability, and desire. Sometimes he won't even have the right kind of conformation. He's what we call a freak. Since he's so unusual, there's no way you can look for his kind. It's better—and a lot easier—to start with the right breeding, then look for the right kind for conformation.

Generally speaking, you don't want a halter-horse type. You see very few top halter horses in performance classes today because they are too heavily muscled to be athletic, or because they are not pretty movers. Look at defensive linemen and compare them to track and basketball players; linemen can't begin to run and turn around and jump like those other guys can. You can make the same analogy between halter horses and performance horses.

The reining prospect must be structurally sound. He cannot have many major faults such as crooked legs, too straight in the hocks, a short thick neck, a long back, and weak loins. He's got to look like he has the strength, agility, and other features it takes to make a great reining horse.

These are only generalities, however, because a horse with a great mind and a great heart can overcome some physically limiting factors. But you can't tell what kind of heart and mind he has until he's old enough to ride...and sometimes you have only a short time to look at a prospect. So you must have some general guidelines to follow.

One of them is size. I like an average-size horse, say 14-3 to 15-1 hands. A horse that's too small doesn't have the stamina and strength it takes to show in reining over a long period of time. By a small horse, I mean one that stands maybe 14-2 and has small bones. He will be more prone to break down.

Now, I know a lot of people will say little horses can be tough, but they're probably talking about stamina for endurance. I'm using the term small as it relates to muscle and bone structure, and their ability to withstand the physical stress to which a reining horse is subjected.

A horse that's too large doesn't have the quickness and agility that he should. Again, this is a generality because there are some 16-hand horses that are pretty movers and can stop and turn around better than some smaller horses, but they are the exception and not the rule. Horses with massive muscles, thick and heavy shoulders, and a wide front end do not adapt well to this event.

The reining prospect should have adequate bone to stay sound, and a good-size foot to avoid problems like navicular. Ideally his legs should be straight. It doesn't hurt if he toes out a little in front, but if he's toed way out, he can't gallop as pretty, and probably can't turn around as pretty because his front feet interfere with each other. Toeing-in is not good either, as this will decrease the stride length when the horse is trying to turn around (spin); the front legs can't cross over like they should.

Expensive Hobby, one of the greatest reining horses in history, was built the way I like a reining horse to be put together. He was formally retired in May 1983.
Don Trout Photo

"I *love* a horse that's strong in the stifle. He can get into the ground and stop, and hold his stop in any kind of ground."

Dust billows as Expensive Hobby reaches the end of a long slide.

To be a good stopper, a horse must be structurally correct behind. The hocks should be strong, durable, and well made because of the great stress placed on them when the horse stops.

Looking at the hocks from the side, they should be correct, but I don't mind if they have a little bend in them so they are slightly sickle-hocked. I'd prefer that over being too straight in the hocks. You also have to look at where the hocks are in relation to an imaginary plumb line dropped from the point of the buttocks. A horse can be sickle-hocked, but with his hocks out behind him because he's too long between the stifle and the hock; he's not going to be much of a stopper. However, if his hocks are under him and have a little bend, he's already in a semi-stopping position.

From the rear, the hocks should be straight to provide the strength the horse needs for stopping, although I've had some pretty good stoppers that were a little cow-hocked, or bow-legged. You would think they couldn't hold a slide—that their legs would splay out or cross, but it's amazing what some of these crooked-legged horses can do.

If we were to draw the perfect reining horse, we'd draw one with powerful hindquarters; they are the basis of a reining horse because he's got to use his hind end, and to do so, he needs power—lots of it. We want one with plenty of muscle in the hindquarters, but not over-muscling, like the massive muscling in some halter horses. We want long, strong muscling through the hip and down into the stifle, especially the inside of the gaskin and stifle. I *love* a horse that's strong in the stifle. He can get into the ground and stop, and he can hold his stop in any kind of ground.

A horse with a weak stifle may be able to slide along the surface, but he can't get in the ground. He is also more apt to injure himself in the stifle.

My kind of horse should also have a long hip and a strong loin. I like a reining horse to break in the loin when he stops so he can really get in the ground and push with his hindquarters. He's got to push his back feet forward in order to balance himself as his momentum shifts from his forehand to his hindquarters as he stops. He can't do this with a weak loin.

His back should be medium in length—not too short because it needs some length for flexibility to arc or bend properly, and not too long because then it's difficult for the horse to control, and lacks strength.

The horse definitely should have good withers to keep the saddle in the middle of the back. Very few great stopping horses have mutton withers. I'm not sure why, but I think it has to do with overall structure and strength. The best horses are what I call slave-looking—with a big hip, powerful stifle, medium back, and good withers. They all tie together. Plus good withers usually go along with a good neck. Look at mutton-withered horses and you'll find very few with well-shaped, flexible-type necks.

I like a neck whose top line flows into the poll, so the poll has some curve to it instead of being flat and stiff. That kind of poll won't have any release to it since it can't flex easily. The bottom of the neck should make a straight line to the throatlatch and not be what's called an upside-down neck. The neck should also come out of the shoulders just right—not too low, not too high. And, of course, you don't want a ewe-neck.

I don't want an excessively long neck on a reining horse because you lose some control. When I touch the horse on the neck with the rein, I want his head, poll, crest—his entire neck—to turn. If the neck's excessively long, the total neck might not be as controllable as I want it to be.

I don't want a short neck, or a thick neck, because they lack flexibility; those necks don't bend laterally or vertically like they should. The best kind of neck is refined, and medium in length.

Ideally, the shoulder line should be sloping, but to me, the most important feature about the shoulder is its size. A horse with massive, heavily-muscled shoulders with the legs out on the points lacks agility and handiness. So does a horse with a wide chest. He can't cross over with his front legs when he turns around, and he won't have the "athletic reach" it takes to stretch out in the rundown, and then use his front legs properly in the stop. But I don't want the horse pinched in the chest, either. He needs a pretty good V so he has enough width to move well, but not so much

"Very few great stopping horses have mutton withers. I'm not sure why, but I think it has to do with overall structure and strength."

width he moves like a truck.

It doesn't make much difference how pretty the head is on a reining horse, but personally, I like to ride a good-looking horse, and sometimes he can add to your score. If a judge has two horses that work about equally, but one's prettier than the other, the better-looker will probably win. However, "pretty is as pretty does!"

Contrary to what some people think, I don't believe there's any correlation between a pretty head and a lot of intelligence. There are many horses with beautiful heads that are empty between the ears.

I do believe that the length of the mouth affects how good a horse might be as a reiner. When a horse has a long mouth, often he's the kind that will open his mouth when you pull on the bridle. Usually he has a tall roof to his mouth, too, and won't be as sensitive in the bridle. And if he has a stout lower jaw, he might take ahold of the bridle and

pull on you.

A horse with a shallow mouth usually has the capability to carry a bridle (bit) better, and also be more responsive to the bit because he will generally have a lower roof to his mouth. To explain this a little better, I like to use bits with high-enough ports so they work off the roof of the mouth as well as the bars and the chin groove. Then when I simply pick up the reins, that signals the horse that I'm going to ask him to do something because he feels the port move in his mouth. That allows me to take a lighter hold of his chin (with the curb strap). When a horse is alerted that you're going to ask him to do something, he's ready and responds more quickly and smoothly. You can't get this effect when using a bit with a straight bar or Sweetwater port, or on a horse that has a tall roof to his mouth.

Another factor to keep in mind, even though it's not all that important, is the thickness of the lips. A horse with thick lips or a fat muzzle isn't as sensitive and won't respond to the bit as well. It's just like a horse with thin skin; you don't have to cue him as firmly as one with a thick hide.

As for color, a good horse is a good horse. Some of the greatest horses in the business today are bays, chestnuts, and sorrels...probably because there are more horses of those colors. But I've had some good gray horses, and some great palominos and buckskins. It doesn't bother me what color a horse is as long as his mind and heart are in the right places, and those are the hardest factors to determine. We can't judge them until we can ride the horse, although we can get a general idea by working with him from the ground. If he's bull-headed or ill-tempered during halter-breaking and other early handling, he'll probably be that way under saddle.

When it's possible, I like to turn a young horse loose in a pen and watch him move. If he's in a group in a pen or pasture, I try to get him away from the others—like in a round corral. Usually the better horses have a spark to 'em, with a good look in their eyes; they are inquisitive, but a little leary of what's going on. They will stand quietly, but when you move at 'em, they jump away quick, then stop and turn around to see

Expensive Hobby always stayed elevated and flexible in front during a stop.

what you're doing. Those that just stand there and look at you, or turn tail and keep on running, will seldom make good reining horses.

If I were to profile my ideal reining horse, it would have to be Expensive Hobby. When he was three years old, I bought him for Georganna Stewart Shelley as a reining horse prospect because he fit the mold I like. Since he turned out to be one of the greatest reining horses in the country, he proved those ideals to be correct.

Overall, he's not what you'd call a real attractive horse. But pretty is as pretty does, and when he was doing his thing, he was a big, stout, powerful, well-oiled piece of machinery. When people saw him unsaddled, standing quietly or resting in his stall, they were surprised be-

cause he didn't look like the same horse they saw in the arena.

When you stand back and analyze him, though, he's got everything I like. He's the right size, standing 15-1 hands; he's not too wide in front; he's got a shallow mouth and nice big eyes; his ears set good; he's got a nice neck and a good set of withers; his back is just the right length; he's strong through the loins; he's got a big, long hip and good tailset; he's big and powerful in the hindquarters and really stout in the stifle; he's got fancy hocks that are big, strong, close to the ground and set under him just right; and he's got a flexible, physical look about him. To add icing to the cake, he has the right kind of mind and heart; he's solid, dependable, and honest...and he's one in a million!

"If I were to profile my ideal reining horse, it would have to be Expensive Hobby."

A great photo showing the extraordinary reach Expensive Hobby had when turning around. He could turn around faster than any horse I've ever ridden, yet he always maintained correct form.

2   EQUIPMENT

I am very particular about the type of equipment I use because it can make a definite difference in my safety, the horse's comfort, and how we both perform. If, for example, the saddle doesn't fit a rider properly, he can't ride to the best of his ability and therefore he will inhibit what the horse is trying to do. Or, if the horse is irritated by something pinching or rubbing him, he can't be expected to perform well.

Bridles

I prefer all of my work headstalls to be made of good-quality leather with both a browband and throatlatch. I don't like most one-ear bridles for two reasons: 1) they sometimes allow the bit to lie crooked (one side higher than the other) in the horse's mouth, and 2) sometimes when you're riding with a snaffle and pull the reins, the action of the bit causes the bridle to press on the ear at the same time. That's not good.

I do ride most of my bridle horses in a split-ear headstall, but the ear piece is made properly. It should either be made of sufficient size and be adjustable, or it should be slit properly so it fits properly, allowing the bit to hang straight.

I like good leather for stoutness and safety. Headstalls and other leather equipment should also last a long time for economy reasons. Every time I put a bridle on a horse, I give it a quick glance to check it for safety. Except for some of my show reins, I secure all reins with leather thongs. I try not to use snaps or buckles because they are liable to come loose just at the moment you need them the most. However, most romal show reins are made with snaps for convenience, and it's difficult to change them.

I like to use a leather chin strap on a snaffle to keep it from sliding through the mouth; it applies no pressure. And I fasten it so it's below the reins. On fin-

ished horses that are straight up in the bridle, I'll use a leather chin strap or a chain curb, depending on which the horse needs. Horses that are real light and sensitive in the mouth generally only need a leather chin strap; this preserves the sensitivity of the chin groove.

Reins

On my snaffle bridles, I ride with 3/4-inch to 1-inch reins made of good English-type leather. I've tried the flat-braided nylon reins, but I don't think they maintain the consistency in weight and substance that leather reins do. New reins made of good leather are a little firm, but they limber up into nice, well-oiled reins that you can use for several years, and that have a lot of balance and feel to both you and your horse.

A silver bit hanger on a show headstall.

14

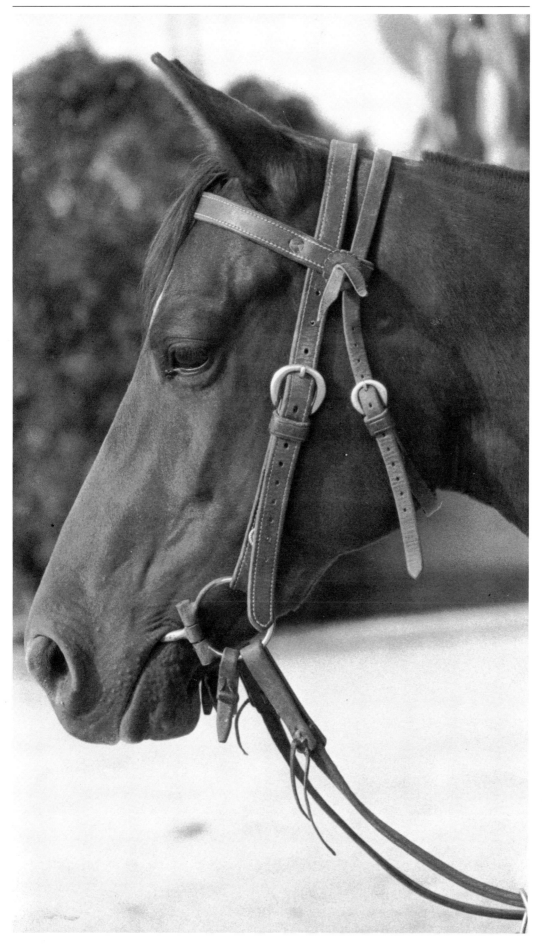

A work headstall with my favorite snaffle bit. The length of the headstall should be adjusted as shown, so the snaffle puts at least one wrinkle in the corner of the mouth.

A Dave Murray bit with a frog mouth-piece that I primarily use on pleasure horses.

To have this *feel*, they should be medium in weight. I don't think the horse can feel a light, shoestring-type of rein against his neck, and the rider can't feel it in his hand either. Since a really heavy rein can be awkward to handle, I opt for the medium-weight reins. I never use weighted reins of any kind.

Bits

This will have to be brief because we could write an entire book on bits alone. Like most trainers, I have acquired a number of bits—snaffles, curbs, half-breeds, spades—over the years, and a sampling of my favorites are shown in the accompanying photos. Which bit I use on a particular horse depends on the horse and his particular needs. Is he light in the mouth? Or does he tend to get a little heavy and therefore need a bit with more leverage and weight? You also have to find a bit that a horse is happy with. Bits are a lot like shoes, or boots. You can walk okay in a lot of boots, but some are far more comfortable than oth-

A bit that I won as a trophy in 1971 with Pink Pony; it was a year-end award in the Arizona Quarter Horse Breeders Association. It has Santa Barbara cheeks and a modified Salinas mouthpiece, which is shown on the next page.

An interior view of the tack room where we keep the work equipment we use every day.

"You also have to find a bit that the horse is happy with."

A modified Salinas mouthpiece with Santa Barbara cheeks (shown on preceding page). This is the bit I used on Expensive Hobby most of the time—with a leather curb strap.

A mild half-breed bit.

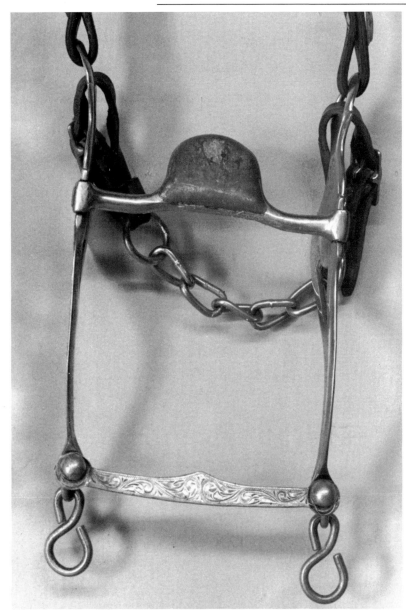

The Mona Lisa was designed by Don Dodge years ago, and he named it after one of his best bridle horses.

A low Salinas mouthpiece.

A Salinas mouthpiece.

ers. Bits feel the same way to a horse.

I have several bits which I use frequently, and the Mona Lisa, Salinas, San Joaquin, and grazer are probably my favorites. My least favorite bit is the straight bar, or Mullen mouth, because it gives the horse no signal, or warning, before the chin strap hits him.

I do have a couple of spade bits, and I use them mainly for bitting up horses. I take the chin strap off, take the slack out of the reins and tie them around the saddle horn, and let the horse stand in his stall. When he sticks his nose out or leans on the bit, the mouthpiece rises up and presses against the roof of his mouth. He learns that when he brings his nose or head back down, the pressure is relieved. It teaches him not to lean on the bit, and it's a good way to use a spade.

I take the curb strap off for two reasons: 1) I'm trying to teach him to learn to respond to pressure from the bit, not the curb strap, and 2) I'm trying to preserve the sensitivity in the chin groove as much as I can. I don't believe in roughing up that area and getting it calloused,

because then it won't be as responsive to the chin strap.

I seldom ever show a horse in a spade because it takes a great deal of time to prepare a horse to pack one properly. Also, with my techniques, I've never felt the need to use one. I don't feel any of the great horses I have ridden would have shown any better.

The snaffle is the basis for just about all of my training. I like a smooth snaffle with a 3/8-inch mouthpiece made of iron. As a matter of fact, I believe iron, or cold steel, works better in a horse's mouth than anything else, aluminum and stainless steel included.

Iron will rust, and it keeps a little sweeter mouth on the horse.

There is a time to use copper in the horse's mouth; copper will enhance the flow of saliva, which helps keep the mouth moist and therefore softer. In the old days I always heard that a horse who slobbers is a horse with a good mouth, and I'll go along with that.

Copper used by itself is too soft, and a horse could chew through the mouthpiece of a snaffle made with straight cop-

"The snaffle is the basis for just about all of my training."

A twisted copper-wire snaffle made with an iron core.

An assortment of cavessons made from half-inch nylon rope.

"Once a horse is broke, he should feel you picking up the reins and start his reaction before you ever take hold of him."

This is my favorite snaffle bit and it was designed by Don Dodge so it doesn't pinch the corners of the mouth. I have a number of these snaffles, including some made with twisted-wire mouthpieces.

per. The best copper-mouthed snaffles have an iron core with copper over the top.

My twisted-wire snaffles are made that way, and I like them because I get a better *feel* from a copper twist than I do a steel twist. That's just a personal preference. Other people might get along fine with an iron twisted-wire snaffle, the way some people get along pretty good with stainless steel bits. But I don't, and I don't recommend them.

My favorite snaffle was designed by Don Dodge. I like it because it doesn't pinch the horse in the corners of the mouth, and because it has a little bit of weight to it; when you drop the reins, it

drops away from the horse. He can feel it better. With a real light bit, he doesn't know where it is; that is, he can't easily tell when you have contact on the reins, or when you turn them loose.

Once a horse is broke, he should feel you picking up the reins and start his reaction before you ever take hold of him, if you are using the right kind of bit with the right reins, and know how to use them. But you can't get this done with a lightweight bit and reins—the horse simply can't feel them.

Running Martingale

There's only one kind I like; it's made

out of leather, and it's a regular running martingale, not a rig you attach to a breast collar. This one snaps into a ring in the cinch, and has a neck strap. It's also plenty long so it doesn't inhibit the horse until he gets his head out of position.

If a martingale is always pulling the head down, it's putting constant pressure on the bit, which is bad, and it doesn't allow the horse to develop his natural head position. We like our horses to carry their heads somewhere between where it's natural for them, and vertical to the ground. If you force a horse into a totally unnatural position, he's not going to be happy or comfortable.

On the other hand, if the martingale is too long, it doesn't do any good. I like to adjust mine so the rings come to the middle of the neck if you pull them straight up; or if you pull them toward the head,

I adjust a running martingale so the rings come within an inch or two of the throatlatch when they are pulled toward the head.

Another view showing the length I like on a running martingale. It also shows a breast collar, which I always use to help keep the saddle in position.

21

"A well-made saddle also tends to stay more secure on the horse without having to cinch him so tight."

they should come within an inch or two of the throatlatch.

Saddle Blankets

I use a fleece pad because it is comfortable for the horse with something like a double Navajo on top of it. Sometimes a hair pad will irritate a horse with thin skin. When fleece pads are new, they can be a little slippery, but after they're broke in, I never have trouble with them...if the horse has the right kind of withers, and if I have the right kind of saddle that fits well, and if it's cinched up properly.

This combination—fleece-type pad and double Navajo—sits the saddle on the back properly; it keeps the saddle off the withers, yet doesn't put it too far away from the back. I want to ride fairly close to the horse's back.

I know a lot of horsemen think there's no substitute for using a Navajo next to the horse's back, but because Navajos absorb so much sweat, I feel they get too stiff and rough. They're not easy to clean, either. And because of the way they are woven, they tend to curl up a

little bit and could possibly bind under the saddle. Besides, a good Navajo is awfully expensive!

Saddles

I ride what I call a stock saddle, and I use it for everything. My saddles sit fairly low on the horse's back, and weigh 50 pounds or maybe even a little more. I like a good, sturdy saddle for safety and comfort...I don't think a lightweight saddle would have the quality of leather I like. A well-made saddle also tends to stay more secure on the horse without having to cinch him so tight. I only take one wrap when I cinch up so there's no bulk under my legs, which allows me to move them freely.

I don't think weight, per se, bothers a horse, not even a two-year-old. If he has the size and stamina to be ridden, he can pack the weight of a saddle okay. But weight does become a factor when, say, a 200-pound man on a 900-pound horse rides like a sack of potatoes, or if the saddle doesn't fit the horse properly, or if the saddle is setting too far forward over the withers, or too far back. Then

Some of the saddles, blankets, and snaffles we use every day.

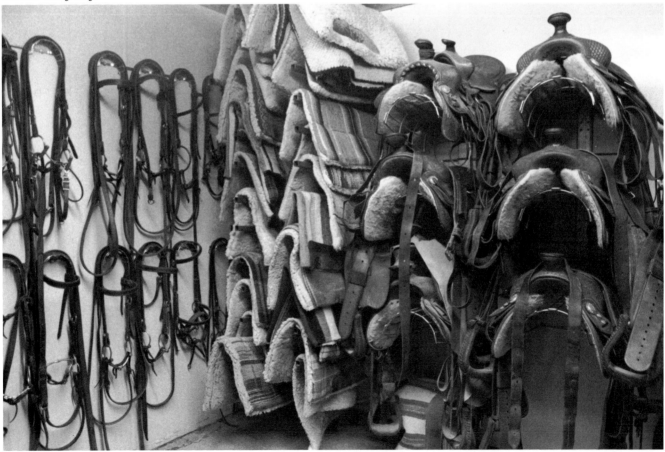

Expensive Hobby, saddled and ready to go. I always check my equipment before making a run, and this photo was taken in February '83 just before we did dry work and cow work for the AQHA film, Working Cow Horse.

weight is critical.

I like a saddle with at least a 2 1/2- or 3-inch cantle, and a seat that is comfortable and helps me sit securely, but which also allows me to move back and forth a little. Some saddles have such a deep seat you can't move, and that's not good because there are times when you need to shift your weight. I like moderate swells, and a horn that's low. If it's high, then you have to raise your hand too high to rein your horse.

All my saddles are full-double rigs. I believe in a back cinch, and in keeping it snugged up right next to the belly to keep the saddle down on the back. That's important because of some of the maneuvers we ask our horses to do; they can perform better if the saddle isn't bouncing up and down.

I like standard stirrups with a tread of 2 1/2 or 3 inches. I don't want them any wider because that makes them heavier, and too easy to lose. When I have to spur a horse, I want to move my feet quickly, and I can't do it with a heavy stirrup.

If a stirrup's too narrow, I think it tends to make you ride with your toes down, and I like my heels down. That's better horsemanship…but I will say there are some great riders who ride with their toes down, and I wouldn't begin to tell them to change their style! But most people will have better luck if they stick to what's been proven as good horsemanship.

I don't like oxbow stirrups, even for cutting, because they hurt the sides of my feet, and because I like a flat platform on which to put my feet.

Hackamores

The bosals of my hackamores vary from 1/4-inch to 1-inch in diameter. Almost all of them have a rawhide core with a rawhide or latigo cover. Since latigo is softer, I use those bosals on a more sensitive horse. I like a long bosal (12-inch) with a good-size heel knot so the bosal will drop away from the jaw when the pressure is released.

That's why I also like some weight to my bosals. In addition, the giving and taking of the bosal (pulling and releasing) has a tendency to help set the head; when the bosal rocks on the nose, it will

"I believe in a back cinch, and in keeping it snugged up right next to the belly to keep the saddle down on the back."

23

"...a large bosal is not necessarily more severe."

bring the head in.

Which bosal to use depends on the rider's preference and the individual horse, but one thing to keep in mind is that a large bosal is not necessarily more severe. Sometimes a rawhide bosal that's small, but stiff, will really bite a horse, and we don't want that because it will make a horse resistant.

I like a little bigger bosal, a 5/8ths or 3/4-inch, that's a little softer so the horse won't resist it. A real big bosal, a 1-inch, in my opinion is best for a big horse, or one that's maybe heavy-headed. He lacks sensitivity and needs to be bumped a little harder. Sometimes I'll also use a big bosal on a young horse. I want it to bounce around on his head so he can find a comfortable position to carry his head so the bosal doesn't bounce.

I don't use a complete hackamore headstall with fiador, etc., because I don't think it's necessary. Also, sometimes a fiador prevents the bosal from dropping away from the head when I release the pressure.

All of my hackamore reins (mecates)

A smooth latigo bosal, 5/8ths inch in diameter.

Some of the hackamores in my collection—plus skidboots, hobbles, a reata, mecates ("McCartys"), and catch ropes.

are made of mane hair, except for a few that have tail hairs mixed in, and they are approximately 22 feet long.

Cavessons

There are times when I want to put something on a horse to help him learn to keep his mouth shut. For this, I like to use nylon rope, about a half-inch in diameter, and with a barrel knot tied at the bottom, or at the heel.

I adjust it so it hangs just below the bridge of the nose, and so I can fit two fingers underneath it. That allows him to crack his mouth, but if he opens it wide, the cavesson takes hold of him and discourages him from doing it.

Protective Boots

I always use splint boots for two reasons: 1) they protect a horse from hurting himself, and 2) they provide some leg support if you use the right kind of splint

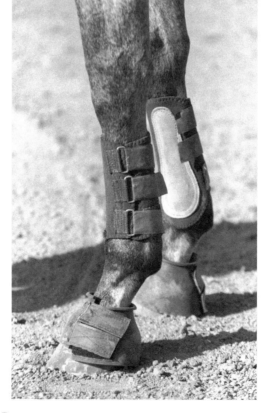

A rawhide bosal that's big, long, and somewhat heavy. This photo also shows the simple piece of leather I use with a bosal instead of a complete hackamore headstall. The thong around the jaw keeps the headstall (hanger) away from the eyes.

Splint boots and bell boots.

"I don't think a horse can perform properly if he's hurt, or if he's afraid he might hurt himself."

boots and put them on properly. They should have about the same amount of tension as you put on a leg wrap. They shouldn't be so tight that they might bow a tendon, but not so loose that they rub sores.

If a horse is inclined to hit a front foot with a back foot, I'll put bell boots on him. I don't think a horse can perform properly if he's hurt, or if he's afraid he might hurt himself.

I always use skidboots when I'm stopping a horse, and there's a particular kind I like. It has a good-size cup, a neoprene cover, and a thick layer of foam rubber on the inside next to the fetlock. I don't like sheepskin lining because dirt and rocks will adhere to it and hurt the horse. With the kind of boots I use, they'll fall out. I don't fasten the bottom strap too tight for the same reason— anything that gets into the skidboot can fall right out.

I never ride a horse with leg wraps on, and I don't believe anyone should unless he's an expert on wrapping legs. Then he will know how to wrap them so they apply uniform pressure, will not injure a tendon or ligament, and will not allow dirt to get under them.

The skidboots I prefer have good-sized cups, neoprene covers, and thick foam rubber on the inside. This photo also shows how we like to trim the back feet on a reining horse. The angle of the toe should correspond with that of the pastern, and the heel is low so the horse can get into the ground better when he stops. On the front feet, we like a little more height to the heel, with the toes trimmed off a bit. Long toes and low heels make it harder for the horse to turn around (in a spin); it's difficult for him to pick up and move his front feet quickly.

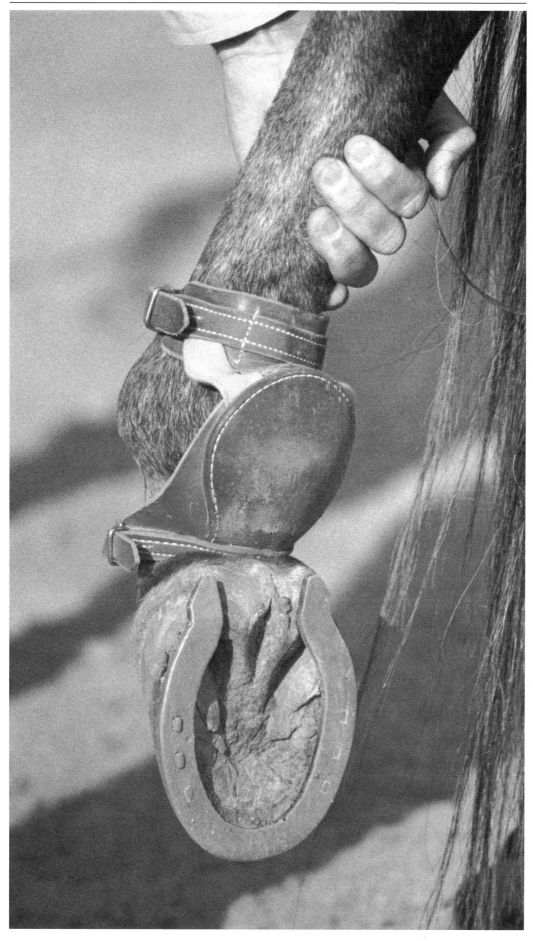

The basic sliding shoe we use is a flat plate that has no drag, and is 3/4 of an inch wide. The trailers are only long enough to protect the bulbs of the heel, and to facilitate sliding. Note that the outside trailer is turned up just a hair; that initiates drag on the inside to prevent the horse from splaying out while sliding. The toe is also rolled up slightly to aid sliding. My horseshoer custom-makes his own shoes so he can punch the holes where he knows a particular horse's foot is the strongest to best hold the shoe. Generally he only uses six nails, and rarely puts nails in the heel area because the heel should not be constricted in any way (to prevent contracted heels). The front feet are usually shod with regular plates, but sometimes we'll use half-round shoes. They reduce the chance of injury if a horse tends to hit himself on the inside leg as he turns around, and they also help a horse to break over more easily. Obviously, a horse must break over with the front feet very quickly in a turn-around. The two men who have shod all of my good reining horses are Charlie Brown and Chuck Waltz, both of the Phoenix area. If a horse is having a problem stopping, I'll run and slide him a few times in the arena to lay some tracks; then the shoer and I will study those tracks to determine what the horse needs to help him, and then we'll adjust the shoes accordingly.

3

ROUND CORRAL & ARENA

Posts in the round corral are angled out slightly.

A round corral is a big help in starting colts, and it should be a minimum of 50 feet in diameter, and a maximum of 100 feet. Mine is 60 feet across, and it's ideal for starting colts because they have enough room to move freely, yet it's not too big. When you're gyping (longeing) the horse free, you can easily keep him going with a longeing whip. In a 100-foot corral, you'd have to run a lot.

My corral is built of telephone poles (for posts) and 2x8s, and the footing is sandy, making it loose and soft in case a rider falls, and providing good footing. Yet it's not so deep it stresses a horse's tendons, ligaments, or muscles.

The sides are seven feet high, and are angled out slightly, reducing the chance of a rider scraping his knees. Some trainers like solid walls so the horse can't see out, and I agree with that to a point. You can keep the colt's attention on you if he isn't distracted by what's going on outside. Plus, with a horse that's pretty rank, if he could see out, that son-of-a-gun might try to jump out.

But I spaced my boards about two or three inches apart, partly to keep it a little cooler in the summer (not everyone has to contend with our kind of weather), and partly to allow you to scramble out over the top if necessary. (The door is solid and can't be opened in a hurry.)

For added safety, we have secured conveyor belting to the lower three feet of the sides. That might help prevent injury to a horse who gets moving so fast he has a tendency to scramble against the walls. It will help protect the walls, too.

My arena is big, measuring 300 feet long and 120 feet wide, with pipe fencing around it. I made it extra large for several reasons: 1) several riders can work in it at the same time without getting in each other's way, 2) there's plenty of length to work horses on the rail before coming to a corner, and 3) there's plenty of room to teach a reining horse to rate his speed—to accelerate, and to slow down.

I pay particular attention to the footing so that it is safe, and provides a good cushion. It has a firm, flat bottom, with two to three inches of a sandy layer on top. That gives a stopping horse something to drive through, allowing him to slide, yet also provides a cushion so he doesn't hurt himself.

Because the footing is good all over, I can stop a reining horse anywhere; he doesn't learn any "sweet spots" where he always expects to be stopped.

Watering the arena minimizes the dust, and keeps the bottom flat and hard. A water pipe with sprinkler heads runs along the fenceline and makes watering easy. After the arena is watered, we work it up lengthwise with a harrow. This works up the top two or three inches to keep the footing level and loose. We also use a drag to keep the surface even.

"...the footing is sandy, making it loose and safe in case a rider falls, and providing good footing."

The sides are seven feet high, and boards are spaced two or three inches apart.

Since the photos for this book were taken, the round corral has been repainted a light tan color, and conveyor belting has been secured to the lower three feet of the sides for safety.

The arena footing is groomed daily.

The arena measures 300 feet long and 120 feet wide.

The hot walker is an indispensable part of our operation.

Controls for the hot walker are located at the gate—and the walker is fenced for safety.

A view of the hot walker and one of our two barns.

"...not everyone
has to contend
with our kind of
weather..."

*Mike Kevil hosing off
a filly he's just ridden.
Except on cold days in
the winter, it's stand-
ard procedure to rinse
off a sweaty horse.*

*Four wash racks are located at the rear of the main barn. The hitchrail on the left can also be used for washing a horse.
Miscellaneous maintenance equipment, winter blankets, etc. are kept in the storage shed at the left rear.*

Cinches are washed regularly to keep them clean.

In the center of the main barn are two grooming and saddling areas, just across the aisle from the tack room where we keep the equipment we use every day.

Mike Kevil walking up the driveway to the main barn after a ride in the desert.

We have a place for everything, and try to keep everything in its place!

4 EQUITATION

Balance is the key to successfully riding a reining horse. For my students to maintain proper balance, I teach them the basic position of sitting almost in the center of the saddle so they are right over the middle of the horse. Both feet should be in the same position in the stirrups, with an equal amount of weight in each. This is the basic position for riding in a straight line, and in circles.

I deviate from this position slightly when turning a horse around, and for stopping. When turning a horse around (spinning), I twist slightly into the turn and keep my inside leg forward. My outside leg is free to move back and "accelerate" the turn-around by bumping the horse with the spur behind the cinch.

When I stop a horse, I like to get down on his back. I push my weight down in the middle in the saddle, but am careful not to lean back too far, or to get my weight on the loins because that would inhibit the horse from stopping properly. I'm also careful to sit right in the middle of the saddle so I don't put more weight on one hind leg than the other.

I've seen some very successful riders make beautiful stops by getting off the horse's back, but for me, my method works better. If you get off the horse's back, that tends to put too much weight on his front end and I feel that decreases the length of his stop. I like to sit down, and actually get a little "behind the motion" of the stop; I like to feel the horse sliding under me.

Those are the three main positions. As for holding the reins, when I was a kid, someone told me, "High hands, high head." I believe that theory, and have stuck with it during my entire career. You should ride with your rein hand no more than two inches above the saddle horn, and when you neck rein, your hand should not move more than six inches either side of the horn. If you have to move your hand more than that, either you're dragging the horse, he's pulling you, or he's not listening. You need to work with him more. When you ask him to stop, your hand should not move more than six inches back. Any more than that and he's not responding properly.

A finished horse should be so responsive to the reins and your body movement that he reacts immediately with very little cue on your part.

I push my weight down in the middle of the saddle when I stop a horse, but am careful not to lean back too far, or to get my weight on the loins.

34

In a turn-around, I twist slightly into the turn and keep my inside leg forward.

I stay right over the middle of the horse when riding in straight lines and circles.

5 BREAKING

"If you do a bad job of breaking, you may create problems that can never be corrected."

We put a tremendous amount of emphasis on starting colts correctly because this foundation lays the groundwork for everything we will teach them, and it will stay with them the rest of their lives. If you do a bad job of breaking, you may never get the problem(s) corrected. I have received several young horses that someone else started and made mistakes with, and I never could develop these horses to their full potential.

Since a good breaking job is so important, we prefer that a young horse not be started if he's coming to us. And if he hasn't been handled much, all the better.

Too much early handling can make a colt cranky, as well as insensitive to cues when we begin riding him. All he needs is to be halter-broke, know how to lead and tie up, and be gentle enough for a little brushing.

I'm using the term "we" because I seldom break colts any more. I'm very fortunate to have a young man named Mike Kevil who does my colt breaking now. He free-lances in the Phoenix area and breaks colts for several people. Another young fellow, Steve Mindak, who has worked for me for years, is also learning to start colts now.

Mike is an exceptional hand, and it's no problem for me to take over a colt he has started because we ride the same and handle the reins the same. There's no basic difference between the way he rides and the way I ride, and that also makes it easy for the colt to adjust when I take over. The big advantage is that it gives me more time to concentrate on the horses that are further along in their training.

The first thing we do with a colt is to make sure he will tie up without pulling back. I think that ninety percent of getting a colt easy to handle is getting him to stand quietly when he's tied. You can

Mike Kevil breaks most of my colts for me.

Mike heading for his "office"—the round corral.

do so much more with him. The key is to frequently tie up a young colt with an unbreakable halter and lead rope to an unbreakable post. That teaches him patience, and that he can't get loose.

We'll tie up a colt and spend some time brushing and handling him, and picking up his feet. The latter is very important so he will stand quietly for the horseshoer. We'll also get him used to having his whiskers and bridlepath clipped, but not his ears. We never clean out the ears until a horse is ready to show.

When we are ready to saddle the colt, we'll tie him to a post in the round corral and sack him out with an old saddle pad. We'll rub him all over with it until he's no longer afraid of it anywhere on his body.

When we feel the colt is ready, we ease the saddle on him, and drop the cinches down quietly on the off side. After adjusting the billet straps so the cinches will fit properly, we cinch up the colt easily. For this, we sometimes have a man on each side if the colt is really nervous. Two men have a better chance of preventing a wreck from happening if the colt gets scared.

We cinch him easily, but if the colt

Steve Mindak will rub this saddle blanket all over the filly before saddling her the first time.

"Too much early handling can make a colt cranky."

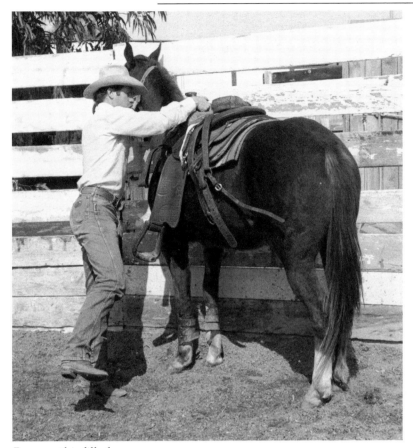

In the next session we'll saddle the colt and gyp (my term for longe) him in the round corral to let him get the kinks out and get used to the saddle. The second or third time, we'll put a snaffle bit on him, slipping the bridle over the halter and tying the reins to the saddle horn with slack in them. We just want him to get used to packing the snaffle.

If the colt is not accepting the snaffle well—chewing on it or throwing his head—we'll put a snaffle on him in his stall and let him live with it in his mouth

Because this filly has already been saddled several times, Mike is more deliberate when he puts the saddle on so she knows it's there.

looks like he's going to blow up, we go right ahead and cinch him up snug. No way do you want a colt half-cinched to rear or jump and have the saddle slide under his belly. Usually a colt will stand and let us cinch him to what I call a medium-snug, meaning it's not going to fall off if he does jump. We pull the back cinch up, leaving it an inch or so from his belly. We don't want it snug against his belly right now, but it shouldn't be so loose he could stick a hind foot in it.

We let the horse stand there a few minutes to think, and then untie him and lead him around. Most of the colts we start are pretty well broke to lead and if one does get excited about being saddled, he's not going to jerk free and run off.

We walk him a little ways, take up the cinch another notch, slap the stirrups against his sides, rub on him, and at times tie him up and leave him saddled for an hour or so.

When we know a colt is a bad one, we'll saddle him, cinch him up snug, and turn him loose and let him pitch all he wants to. When he gets it out of his system, we then proceed with him like we do with the gentle colts.

Steve slips the bridle over the halter.

for a few hours a day. He eats and drinks with it. That usually solves the problem.

Now we begin teaching the colt to bend his neck in response to the bit. We stand beside the colt, take the rein on that side, and pull his head in that direction. If he wants to walk around a little bit, that's okay, as long as he turns his head in the direction you are pulling. We do this several times, and if he responds correctly, we move to the other side and repeat.

If the colt is not bending, we'll tie his head around, first to one side, and then the other, leaving him tied about 30 minutes each way. Say we're tying his head to the left. We put a lot of slack in the

Before he cinches up his filly, Steve shortens the billet strap and adjusts the breast collar so it will fit properly.

This is how we like to tie the head around. The rein is tied to the D-ring of the back cinch so the entire neck must bend. We put a lot of slack in the other rein so it does not prevent the horse from turning his head.

right rein and tie it to the saddle horn, then tie the left rein to the back-cinch D-ring on the saddle. We tie it so the horse is bending his neck about 90 degrees; there's no sense in training a horse to bend more than 90 degrees. We leave the colt in the round pen, and he's free to walk around. Not only does he learn to follow the rein, but he learns to bend his neck and body with the correct arc; he bends his neck from the base up. Later when you get on him, he knows pretty well what you want when you pull the rein.

If a colt is stubborn about bending, we'll tie his head to his tail so that when he fights the pull of the rein, he's fighting himself. The more he pulls against the rein, the more he pulls his tail. After a few minutes of this, he realizes that if he stops pulling, he stops hurting his tail.

Once the colt will bend, is accustomed to packing a saddle and snaffle bit, and knows how to gyp, we take one more step before we drive him. We attach a light cord, about 20 or 25 feet long, to the snaffle, running it through both rings. Then we gyp him with this cord. This teaches the colt to travel with his head a little to the inside, and to stop when he hears "whoa" and feels a light pull on the bit.

The cord has to be light, with no snap, because you don't want any weight on the bit. But you have to be darn careful

Before we drive a colt, we'll gyp him with a light cord attached to both rings of the snaffle.

Because the cord is light, Steve handles it carefully so the filly doesn't get a foot over it.

When Mike drives a colt the first couple of times, he does not run the inside line through the stirrup.

Here, Mike has run the inside line through the stirrup. He stands in the middle of the round corral and drives the filly around the perimeter.

The filly has been traveling to the right; Mike has stopped her and asked her to turn around.

She comes around nicely and breaks into a trot.

that the colt doesn't step over it, especially when you stop him and turn him around. We do this by pulling lightly, so the colt reverses to the inside.

If the colt won't stop in response to this cord, we don't pull harder; instead, we just let him keep going until he's tired and wants to stop. Next time, he'll stop a lot quicker.

When Mike is ready to drive the colt, he does it a little bit differently. He ties the stirrups together, but doesn't run the inside line through the inside stirrup. He leaves that line loose in case the colt gets scared and takes off; Mike can stop him better by pulling his head around with that line. But after the colt has been driven once or twice, Mike will run both lines through the stirrups.

You can drive a colt by walking straight behind him, but we usually stay to the middle of the corral and drive the colt around the perimeter. The inside line will come directly to your hand, and the outside line comes around behind the horse, just above the hocks.

If a colt is nervous or spooky, we might have someone lead him when we first drive him, but this isn't necessary with most colts. While a colt is being driven, he learns that a cluck and some slack in the lines means to move forward; and that whoa and light pressure on the lines means stop. Mike is very careful not to overpull a colt. If he won't stop, Mike just lets him keep going until he's tired and wants to stop. When you stop a colt by using force, you are going

Backing the filly with a light touch.

to create bad mouth problems before you ever get on him. Be patient and give the colt time; he will learn what you want.

One disadvantage of driving a colt is that we can't turn him around the way we'd like to. Ideally, we'd like to have him right next to the fence and turn him sharply to the inside (away from the fence). Having the fence against his rear end would make him plant his hocks when he turns, a basic fundamental for many reining horse maneuvers. We can't do this effectively when we're driving him, but this is a minor detail that can be overcome when we start riding him.

How much time we spend on ground work before we get on a colt can vary widely, depending on the colt. Some are

Mike has several ways of mounting a colt the first time. If he doesn't expect trouble, this is how he does it.

If the colt tends to be broncy, Mike cheeks him while he steps on.

If Mike thinks the colt will explode before he's in the saddle, he hooks his elbow in the left rein to keep the colt's head pulled around for better control.

so gentle that Mike gets on them the first day, and I've even seen him take a colt to the desert on the first day. With colts that are nervous, spooky, or broncy, Mike might spend five or six days on ground work. He wants to be sure he can at least stop and turn a colt before he gets on him.

Once he's mounted, Mike lets the colt move out freely because he wants him relaxed. If a colt wants to buck a little, Mike doesn't pull him up because that gives the colt something to brace on and buck even harder. Instead, Mike slaps him with the reins, lines him out, and lets him move on.

Very few colts today are serious about bucking, so this isn't much of a problem, especially with someone like Mike who, without being immodest, says he has no fear of falling off. "If you do," Mike adds, "you better not get on a colt because your fear will transmit to him and he will tense up. You want the colt relaxed, and so you must be relaxed."

Occasionally, a colt doesn't want to move; he just stands after Mike is in the saddle. Mike will wait on the colt for a few minutes, and if he still doesn't move, will cluck to him and pull his head a little to one side. This usually gets the colt untracked since pulling his head unbalances him.

Mike will walk the colt in both directions, turning him both left and right, and then do the same at the trot. Depending on the colt, he might even ask for a lope this first ride. He asks the colt to move out a little faster by clucking to him and using a little "body English." He doesn't apply leg pressure at this stage because the colt doesn't understand it, nor does he use his spurs. Too much kicking or poking him in the belly will lessen his response later when I start putting some dressage leg on him.

If the colt doesn't respond, Mike will take the end of one rein and sort of "pat" the colt on the rear end with it. If that doesn't work, Mike will whack him down the hind leg with the end of the rein. You can only baby a colt so long, and when you ask him to move faster, he should move faster.

True, you might get more *fast* than you want when you whack him, but he can't go anywhere in the round corral. He can only travel in circles, and he can only go fast for so long.

You have to be a good-enough rider to

*Once he's mounted,
Mike lets the filly
move out freely.*

*Mike is asking the
filly to take a couple
of steps back.*

follow through on what you ask a colt to do. If you continue to let him stop and do what he wants to do, he's going to quickly develop some bad habits that can present a real problem in your training later on.

Besides, one sharp whack down the hindleg is far better than several gentle taps. Those mean nothing, and will only irritate the colt. When you want him to move and ask him by clucking, then reinforce your request with a whack down the hindleg, that's his first inkling that you're the boss, and when you ask him, he'd better respond. Pretty darn quick, all you'll have to do is cluck, and give

him some slack, and he'll go.

Once the colt can walk, trot, and lope both ways, and will stop, back up, and turn around, he's ready to go outside. Depending on the colt, the time he has spent in the round corral ranges from one day to fourteen. Although we like to put a good foundation on our colts, we don't want to stay in the round corral any longer than necessary because the colts will get bored. So we head out to the desert as soon as we feel a colt is ready for it.

After the filly will walk, trot, and lope both ways, she's ready to go outside.

45

6 RIDING OUTSIDE

"Riding a colt outside tells us a lot about him."

When I'm riding outside, there are no horses or fences to distract my colt, and no people or telephones to distract me. Here, I can concentrate.

I am a firm believer in riding horses—from green colts to finished horses—outside, and here in Scottsdale, that means the desert. We are fortunate to still have easy access to a lot of desert country. When I am riding outside, it's just me and my horse. There are no other horses to distract him, no fences for him to rely upon, and no barns for him to drift toward. And there are no people to distract me, and no telephone. Here, I can concentrate.

Riding a colt outside tells us a lot about him—how athletic he is, how smart he is, and if he's trainable. I believe you could ride a horse outside and teach him almost everything he will ever need to know in the show ring, except how to travel along a rail and handle the corners properly.

I even put a snaffle on my older horses and take them outside, and I believe this is a major reason why they stay fresh for years. If you only ride a horse in an arena, he will probably become sour and bored pretty darn fast, and then you might have to use more forceful means to get the same work done.

I realize there are many trainers and riders who have no outside places to

46

There are a lot of sandy paths we use for galloping.

ride, and some do an outstanding job of training. My hat's off to them because I know the problems when you can only ride in an arena.

In the desert is where we start the foundation on our colts, which is the most important aspect of training. As Don Dodge, one of the greats, says, "The foundation isn't just anything; it's everything!"

We like to put a solid foundation on our colts because it gives us something to build on, and something to go back to if need be. As an analogy, consider a pro golfer whose swing suddenly goes awry. What does he do? He slows down, and starts all over with the basics. You do the same thing with a horse if he gets confused, does something wrong, or has a memory lapse.

We begin building this foundation outside. For the first few rides, we leave his

head alone as much as possible; we just ride him. But while we're doing this, we can subtly teach him to travel straight. This is important because straight is the optimum for everything he will have to do in a reining pattern: run-downs, stops, backing, turn-arounds, and even circles.

Teaching a colt to travel straight isn't as easy as it sounds, because most green colts have a tendency to drift or wander. What we do is head toward a fence which is, say, two miles south. We line the colt out in that direction at a brisk trot or even a gallop. As he gets used to packing the weight of a rider, and as he realizes that he will be traveling some

Mike Kevil loping a filly during her first ride outside. He leaves her head alone as much as possible.

The varying terrain helps the filly learn how to handle herself.

"The foundation is the most important aspect of training."

"Riding a colt out-
side helps develop
his coordination
and balance."

distance, he starts moving in a straighter
line.

When we come to some bushes or
trees, we slow down, point him to the
right or left using a direct rein, go
around them, and break off again. This
gives us a chance to improve his steering, and at the same time gives him a
reason for responding to the rein.

If the colt starts to drift too much from
our line of travel, we pick up one rein
lightly, head him back on course, and
slack off on the rein. He learns that when
we are not steering him, he should be
traveling straight and should "stay between the reins."

Riding a colt outside teaches him to
move naturally and how to handle himself. It helps develop his coordination
and balance. He also learns how to move
out and gallop. Many colts that are only
ridden in an arena never have a chance
to learn these things. Their gaits are stiff
and peggy, they don't know how to run,
and if you get them off the rail, they are
lost.

It's like comparing colts raised in big,
rough pastures to colts raised in small
pens. The pasture colts will learn how to
handle themselves at all speeds in different types of terrain. They'll make much
better horses when you start them under

saddle than will those colts that have
been standing in a pen all their lives.

We always ride our colts outside with
a ring snaffle and a running martingale.
The snaffle is the basis for all our training, and we even ride our older horses in
it at times. But we rarely use a cavesson
or anything else to tie the mouth shut.
First of all, I don't think it's such a bad
thing for a colt to open his mouth when
he's pulled on. I think it's better for him
to give his jaw by opening his mouth
than it is to lock up and pull on you.

Second, I don't think it's good to keep
a colt fully contained. If you try to trap
him—in this case by tying his mouth

*Rolling a colt back into a bush tells me a lot
about his suppleness and athletic ability. I'm
between two bushes here.*

*This colt has been rid-
den for several
months and is han-
dling himself well as I
roll him back to the
right with a light pull.*

Backing up is an integral part of the work we do in the desert.

We trot and lope a lot of circles around bushes.

I'm using the inside rein to bring the colt's head in.

The colt is supple, relaxed, and arcing his body nicely.

shut—you create resistance. As I already mentioned, we leave a colt's head alone as much as we can when we first start riding him outside. Later when it comes time to make him do something, we'll teach him to give; that is, flex at the poll and bring his head in with his mouth shut. At first, he might drop his lower jaw first, then bring in his head and close his mouth. But if you are a good rider and have skillful hands, it won't be long before you can pick up the reins and he's going to give his entire head as one unit, not just his lower jaw.

With a real green colt, we concentrate primarily on teaching him to travel straight. As he progresses, we'll start doing more things. When we leave the barn with him, we walk until we get far enough away that we feel his attention

50

When I roll a colt back into a bush and he puts his hocks under him like this, I know he has some athletic ability.

Although we are moving more slowly here, the colt has planted his pivot foot and is going to sweep by the bush correctly.

span is on the rider, rather than on the barn or other influences. Then we might trot him maybe a half mile, and then leg him into a lope.

At this point, we don't care which lead he takes. We just want him to learn to lope with very light contact on the reins; we don't want to pull on his head or leg him off into a specific lead.

When we feel the edge is off him, we'll stop and let him get a little air. Then we start working on specific things, such as teaching him to circle properly at the trot and lope, how to stop, back up, and even turn around. One thing I like to do is turn a colt back into a bush. I'll be trotting or loping around a bush, will ask the colt to stop, and then roll him back (into the bush) and go the other way. This simple maneuver tells me a lot about the colt's suppleness and athletic ability.

If he can plant his hocks and use them, that tells me he'll be able to turn around (spin) and back up pretty easily. If he can handle his front end and sweep across himself, to avoid hitting the bush, that's further proof he has potential. On the other hand, if he just wallows through the middle of the bush, that tells me he might not be such a good prospect.

While riding in the desert, we can teach the colt how to circle properly, to pick up his leads, how to stop and back up, and even how to turn around. We

will go into the details of each maneuver in succeeding chapters, so at this point, I'll wrap up the generalities about the desert riding.

We do this work at a point far enough from the barn so we have the colt's undivided attention. He may not even know in which direction the barn lies. If you're only a quarter-mile or so away, most colts are still thinking barn, and no matter what you're doing, you can feel the colt's body always drifting or leaning toward the barn. You cannot train him to use his body properly when he's doing this, so ride him farther out.

While we're riding outside, we're careful never to get in a fight with the colt, or get in a situation where we have to really get after him. We want his outside riding to be a relaxing, learning experience for him.

When we head back to the barn, never do we lope or gallop because this teaches him a bad habit, and later we'd have to force him to walk. We'll trot about halfway back, and then walk. We want to instill in him that going outside is pleasant, and that when going back, he should stay relaxed.

7 BACKING

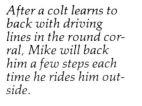

After a colt learns to back with driving lines in the round corral, Mike will back him a few steps each time he rides him outside.

I cannot stress enough how important backing is. Not only because it's a maneuver in itself that a reining horse must accomplish well, but also because it teaches a horse how to use his hindquarters, and therefore plays a key role in the horse's learning how to stop, and how to turn around correctly. In addition, backing helps to develop the mouth, and helps put rate, or control, on the horse.

Many horses have trouble learning to back, and many riders have trouble teaching their horses to back, partly because they are not sure what to do when a horse refuses to back. If it's a horse that has never had the proper foundation in training, such as learning to give to the bit, or has bad habits such as throwing his head up, the rider has added woes. The only solution: go back to the basics, because if you cannot get a horse to back, you're in trouble. Forget everything else until you fix this problem.

For some horses, backing is difficult because it's an unnatural movement. The added weight of a rider compounds the problem, especially on a young horse. In order to move in reverse, the horse must make his back convex, and it can be hard for some colts to do this until they are more accustomed to packing the weight of a rider.

They've got to learn, however, because a reining horse must be able to use his hindquarters properly. Backing teaches him this.

I'll start teaching a colt to back while just casually riding him in the arena. I'll bend his head around, then stop and ask him to back a few steps. I don't make a big production out of it. Then I'll move him on forward again, bend him a little bit, and then stop and ask him to back a few steps.

When I ask him to back, I take the slack out of both reins; then keep one hand stationary and pull lightly with the other. This uneven pressure unbalances him so it's harder for him to resist backing up.

I don't put constant pressure on the bit, because the horse can set his jaw against it; and I don't like to use a see-saw motion because that can cause the head to go up.

If the colt does resist backing, I'll usually dismount and tie his head around for a little while. This will soften up the corners of his mouth and develop some lateral flexibility so he will handle better—and when a colt handles better, he will usually back up better.

Keeping one hand stationary while I pull lightly with the other might cause him to back with his body crooked. Straight, of course, is the optimum, but if the colt backs a little crooked at this stage, it's no big deal and I can realign

"Backing plays a key role in the horse learning how to stop."

A colt must be able to easily give his head in both directions before you ask him to back. This develops his lateral flexibility.

I'm suppling (bending) this filly while she backs to make her give her body. This helps develop overall flexibility, and makes her give her head. She's just starting to give her head here.

As she begins to give her head, she is starting to back much more easily.

Now the filly is moving back well with just a light pull.

because it doesn't give the colt time to get set physically and mentally to refuse. As soon as he takes a couple of steps back, I rein him off in another direction right away, go on to another corner, and repeat. After doing this a few times, he'll generally back a lot more easily.

After he develops a reverse gear, I'm content if he will simply take three or four steps back readily. I'll work on the dispatch and distance later.

Occasionally I'll get a horse in that's really stubborn about backing. Often the problem stems from a rider who has pulled and hauled on the reins so much that the horse sets his jaw and refuses to give—as a defensive measure to protect his mouth. Or, maybe it's a horse who just doesn't like to give his head.

With a horse like this, I'll bit him up to soften his mouth. I'll tie each rein straight back to the D-rings on the saddle, and adjust them so that when the horse brings his nose in to the vertical, he gets slack in the reins—and relief from the pressure. For this, I'll turn him loose in the round corral or arena where he can move around, and where we can keep an eye on him.

The average horse will usually only pull on the reins so long before he learns to come off the pressure by himself and give his head. Then he'll be a lot easier to back up.

This would be a good time to mention that if the horse continually resists pressure on the reins by throwing his head up, have a veterinarian check his teeth. He could have wolf teeth or other dental problems.

After I've ridden a colt about 60 days, I start getting him to back farther and more quickly. My goal is to have him immediately start to back as soon as I pick up the reins and pull back lightly. I don't mean run backwards, but to back promptly and smoothly with his head in the correct position, his mouth shut, and his hindquarters under him.

I start this new program by picking up both reins and taking the slack out of them, then adding tension to both reins. If the colt doesn't come back readily, I'll pull one rein harder than the other. This might raise his head somewhat, but occasionally some things must be temporarily altered to correct others. My objective now is to make him move back-

him later.

How far do I ask him to back? Ideally, he should give me as many steps as I want, but right now, I am more concerned that he backs freely and easily than I am with distance. If he does back well, I will only ask for three or four steps. If I know he will only give me three or four, I'll quit asking before he quits backing. It's very important that he learns to keep backing until I ask him to stop; not when he wants to stop.

If a horse is reluctant to back, I'll ride him into a corner of the arena. But I don't casually walk into the corner—I'll drive him in at the trot so he stops with his body bunched up in the backing position. Then I set one hand and give one firm pull back with the other, release it quickly, and repeat. This usually works

With a horse that is reluctant to back, I'll ride him into a corner of the arena.

I'll drive him in at a trot or lope so he stops with his body in the backing position.

This filly stopped crooked, but when I pulled the right rein to straighten her, it also started her backing before she had a chance to resist.

"I'll quit asking him to back before he quits backing."

After the filly backs a few steps, I'll rein her off in another direction and repeat this exercise in another corner.

"Backing also helps put rate, or control, in a horse."

Here, I'm hustling the filly a little bit. I do this with a young horse who is hanging (leaning) on the bit, or who is farther along in his training in order to make him back with more dispatch.

faster. If he comes back pretty good, I'll drop the reins and let him stand for a moment.

Then I'll ask him again. I'll pick up both reins, and if he doesn't want to come back with dispatch, I'll pull one rein harder; I'll put straight back toward my hip, while keeping firm tension on the other rein. When I pull, it's a give-and-take situation. Putting more tension on one rein keeps the colt a little more relaxed and off balance so he will be less likely to take hold of the bit. But I am not see-sawing the reins.

Pretty soon the colt will get the idea that he's supposed to go in a reverse direction with ease. And I want him supple, so he backs fluidly and freely as soon as I pick up the reins and pull lightly. I don't want him scared, with his body tense and stiff. To encourage him to move back a little faster, I might nudge him in the belly with my heel or spur; and I might also cluck to him.

When I cluck to my horses, they know that means I want more out of them. But I never cluck until they are already doing what I ask. For example, I don't cluck for more speed in a back-up until the horse

is already backing. Same with nudging with my heel.

As we already mentioned, backing teaches a colt how to use his hindquarters to stop and turn around. And teaching him to back on a fairly light rein is also helping to develop his mouth. He is learning to *give*—to drop his head and tuck his nose in—as soon as you pick up the reins.

Backing also helps put rate, or control, in a horse. In no way, shape, or form is a good reining horse anything like a barrel horse or any other speed horse that runs wide open. A reining horse is not running a race; he's always moving at a controlled speed, even in his run-downs prior to stopping. Rate in a reining horse is very important, and we start putting rate in a colt right now when we're backing him up. How?

As he backs, he's 1) giving to pressure from the bit and 2) bending his back up (making it convex), which shortens his stride. Later when I'm galloping him and pick up the reins, he's already learned that he gives his mouth and slows down. That's rate. And as he does this, it shortens his stride and makes him arc his

56

Teaching a colt the fundamentals of backing results in a finished horse who backs fluidly with his head in position and mouth closed. This is Expensive Hobby.

back, which gets him to galloping under himself. Then he's in position to stop properly.

At no time when we pick up the reins to slow the horse do we want him to "hollow out"; that is, for his rear end to come up while his back goes down. We want just the opposite: the hindquarters to go down, and the back to round. This is the basis of collection.

As the colt learns to back with dispatch, I pay strict attention to keeping him straight. Two keys to this are keeping the reins absolutely even, so he's getting equal pressure on both sides of his mouth, and keeping my weight equally distributed. It's more difficult for him to back straight if I am leaning to one side.

In theory, the horse should back straight if the reins are even and his body is straight when he starts. But he may have a crook in his body after a few steps. To correct this, I like to move his front end over to realign it with the rear end. Say his rear end is going to the right. Using a combination of direct and indirect rein, I'll move his front end over to the right.

Or I might walk him forward a few steps, realign his front with his rear, and start over. With a colt that persistently backs crooked, I might position him alongside a fence. Once he teaches himself to back straight along a fence, it's a lot easier for me to keep him straight when we are away from the fence.

On more advanced horses that back crooked, I can use my legs to straighten them. Say, for example, the rear end is drifting to the left. I can use my left leg to move the rear over to the right, or, I can use my right leg to bump the right shoulder over to the left. I don't use a leg on colts for this purpose until they understand leg pressure; a green colt may move into my leg and compound the problem.

8 LEG CONTROL

Training a colt is just like taking a youngster through school. He starts out in kindergarten, progresses to grade school, then high school, and a few make it to college. Asking a child to do high school work when he hasn't received a grade school foundation is a waste of time and effort. It's the same with colts.

Our colt is in grade school now. He's already learned to back pretty good, and now I want to start putting a little leg on him. I will use leg control to help teach him to pick up his leads, change leads, move forward or back up in a straight line, turn around correctly...the whole nine yards.

I put leg on my colts fairly easily. While I'm walking or trotting, either in the desert or arena, I'll pick up one rein, press it against his neck, apply leg pressure on the same side, and try to get the colt to move over. What I'm trying to teach him is somewhat of a two-track; that's what dressage people call it. But I'm not going to refine it like they do. I two-track a colt just enough to get more control of his body, and to help develop his suppleness and coordination.

Suppose I want to two-track to the

This shows the position of my hands and leg for two-tracking to the left. I've got the mare's head turned a few degrees to the right, the right rein is laying against her neck, and I've got my right leg against her side.

Two-tracking to the right. I'm keeping just enough tension on the right rein so she can't turn her head any far-ther to the left.

left. I'll pick the slack out of my right rein, press it against his neck, press my right leg against him, and maybe bump him with my heel. (I do just the opposite to two-track to the right.) His natural re-action will be to turn his head to the right, but I don't want him to. So I put just enough tension on the left rein to keep his head straight. He can turn it a degree or two to the right, but no more.

Once the colt has the idea to move away from my leg, the next step is to make him more responsive. I do this by

teaching him to side-pass. Some people teach the side-pass first, then the two-track. But I prefer to teach the two-track first because it uses forward motion and this gives the colt more time to adjust, as it gives him somewhere to go.

For the side-pass, I position the horse facing a high fence, one that he can't get his head over. To go to the left, I do the same thing as before: pick up the right rein, lay it against his neck, hold the left rein to keep his head straight, and press my right leg against him, and keep my

"Keep your non-pressure leg well away from the horse."

Side-passing to the right, using the fence as an aid. I'm pushing her to the right with my left leg.

left leg well away from him.

I use the fence to keep the horse from moving forward; what I've got to do is show him that he can get away from the pressure by moving to the left. As soon as he takes a step or two, I stop and pat him. But if he doesn't move, I'll increase the pressure from my right leg, and maybe kick him a few times if need be. The fence will be there to contain him, and he should move sideways.

He might back up and if he does, I'll drive him forward with both legs, or maybe swat him with a rein. Once he's back to the fence, he's got to go sideways.

Try to prevent mistakes when teaching a horse to side-pass and two-track. For example, keep your non-pressure leg well away from the horse. Some riders unknowingly apply pressure from that leg also, and the result is a confused horse. Stick your non-pressure leg well out to the side—exaggerate if you have to.

Don't ask the horse to go too far too soon. As soon as the horse takes just one or two steps, it's important that you release the pressure and reward him. This tells him he's doing what you are asking. If you don't, and keep pressuring him to move, he's going to get confused.

Don't allow the horse to back up. This happens when the rider is not forceful enough to make the horse move to the side.

Now that we've got this colt backing and side-passing well, let's get him circling properly.

This is more of a finished side-pass, but I'm still using the fence as a barrier. The mare is moving to her left, with her body almost straight, and with no resistance.

9 CIRCLES

Circles are an integral part of the reining pattern, as well as the foundation I like to put on a colt. In a pattern, circles should be more than just a means to an end; that is, to allow a horse to show that he can change leads. Circles reveal the horse's way of going (it should be smooth and pretty), and his ability to follow his nose, stay between the reins, and to travel on the proper lead. When done correctly, circles are a thing of beauty.

I stress circles in my training program for the above reasons, plus the fact that from a circle you can build into other maneuvers. You can work on stopping and backing, turning around, and rolling back to the inside or outside. You can teach a horse to rate his speed—to move on faster or slow down. If he wants to move on too fast, it's easier to teach him to slow down and relax while circling than it is on the straightaway.

Circles, of course, are the basis for figure-8s and learning to change leads. And if you have a solid circling horse, you will probably have a solid lead-changing horse. But you should never ask a horse to change leads until he is deadset solid in his circles.

I never ask a horse to change leads until 1) I can push him in and out of his circles with my leg and put him wherever I want, 2) until I can point him where I want him to go and he'll go there with his head in position and without my having to rein him all the time, and 3) until I can rate his speed. If I ask him to change leads in a figure-8 before I can do those things, I may have problems, and that will ruin his circles. I want the circles to be correct first.

In order to circle, the horse must have a slight arc to his body, but it's very slight; his nose should be to the inside just enough so I can barely see his eye.

His neck should follow his nose, his shoulders should follow his neck, his back should follow his shoulders, and his hindquarters should follow his back—all on the same track. Both shoulders should be straight up, and he should be relaxed and moving on very light contact.

This body position is also the same basic position the horse will use later for more advanced work, like turning around, or blocking a cow on the fence.

No way do I want to see a horse looking well to the inside of the circle with a lot of curvature in his body. That makes his rib cage area push to the outside, making it more difficult for him to maneuver.

Looking to the outside of the circle is also undesirable. That causes his inside shoulder to drop, which in turn causes the rider to lose a lot of control. It also makes him cut his circles down in size, and makes it difficult for him to change leads. He can change leads much easier when his head is straight in front of him. It's also easier for him to change leads when both shoulders are straight up; he can make a faster, smoother, more efficient change, and he will not develop the habit of diving into his lead changes.

To start a colt on circles, I'll pick out a tree or bush that's on level ground and has good footing surrounding it. First at the trot, and later at the lope, we'll go around and 'round that tree in nice, uniform circles. When circling an object, a horse has less tendency to duck to the inside, and it also gives him something to get his bearings on. I think that's important, and it makes it an easy way to teach him to circle correctly.

To keep his body positioned properly, I'll use light rein contact to put his head where I want it, then I ease off. When his head gets out of position, I'll pick up the

Expensive Hobby circling to the left. His nose is slightly to the inside—just enough so I can barely see his inside eye.

Continuing in the same circle shown above, Hobby stays between the reins.

We start a colt circling by trotting and loping around bushes in the desert. This gives the colt something to relate to, which helps teach him to make circles of a uniform size.

This gray mare is showing good form while loping circles in the arena during a schooling session.

reins again and put his head back where it belongs, then ease off. I want him to learn to keep his head where I put it without my having to keep pressure on the reins. If we are circling to the left, I want him to learn that he stays in that circle until I tell him otherwise. That's what I mean when I say I want a horse to "stay between the reins." If you maintain constant rein pressure, when you do release it, it's like releasing a spring. The colt doesn't know where to go. Constant pressure can also cause mouth problems.

I use the outside rein very little, and only when his head goes too far to the inside. I urge him along with my outside foot, which also serves to keep his side in so his body stays in the correct arc.

I'll circle both directions, but never so long that the horse gets bored. After maybe a half-dozen circles one way, I'll straighten him out and head off to another tree or bush and circle the other way a few times.

When I lope him in circles, he's got to pick up the correct lead, but I don't

make a big hassle out of it at this stage. I'll sit down in the saddle to keep my weight in one place; steady his head with both reins, keeping his head straight in front of him or maybe slightly to the inside; bump him with my outside foot or leg; and cluck to him. If he keeps trotting, I take a rein and slap him down the outside rear leg. If you do this, don't lose your cool—just swat him and go on.

Most colts are a little tense or nervous when you start them in circles, partly because they don't know what you want them to do. To get them relaxed, you have to lope a lot of circles of varying sizes and speed. You can do some of this inside the arena, but I like to do most of it outside where I can put more control on the colt because there are no fences, etc. for him to rely on. Then when I do take him inside, it's a lot easier to make uniform circles because I have so much control over the colt.

After several weeks of loping circles, I have taught this colt how to rate his speed, keep his body straight except for a slight arc to the inside, lope different-size circles, and stay between the reins. I also want to be able to move him in and out of the circles. That means that if I touch him with the right rein while we're loping a left-hand circle, he should go to the inside of the circle (make a smaller circle) and still be under complete control. When I take that rein off his neck, he stays between the reins again, while still circling.

(When I touch the horse with the outside rein, I also use the inside rein to keep his head positioned properly, and to help him comprehend. At this stage, he won't respond to a neck rein only.)

One of the things I like to do from a circle is stop and roll-back to the inside. If I'm loping a left-hand circle, I'll stop, back him up a step or two (using both reins), then drop my outside rein at the same time I pull with my inside rein. That rolls him onto the center of the circle. Then I straighten him out, pick up the lope, and go the other way in a nice, fluid motion.

A lot of people roll back to the outside because that "throws" the horse onto the correct lead going the opposite way. On a horse that's broke, you can roll any way you want to and pick up the correct lead. But there's a reason why I like to roll a colt back to the inside: it keeps him on his inside hock. This actually sets him up in the correct position to pick up the new lead; all I have to do is cock his head to the outside. This is also a "building block" that becomes important later when I come across the arena and ask him to change leads the first time. We'll talk about it in that chapter.

Mistakes

There are several mistakes that novice riders tend to make when they break their own colts. Perhaps the most common is teaching the colt to neck rein too soon. A lot of people do this by laying the indirect rein against the neck, then swatting the colt on the same side of the neck with a switch or riding bat.

This will certainly teach the colt to respond to a neck rein, but it ruins his body position. His head will be too far to the inside of the circle; his head and neck will be turning, but the rest of his body can't possibly track correctly. A

horse like this is often called rubber-necked.

I teach my colts to neck-rein v-e-r-y gradually over a long period of time—months and months. After I've been riding a colt several weeks, I'll gently lay the indirect rein against his neck whenever I turn him with the direct rein. Gradually he learns to respond to the indirect rein, but it might be a year or more before I ever ask him to turn from the indirect rein only. Neck reining is just about the last thing I teach.

Another common pitfall when training is to stick your inside hand out to the side and "lead" the horse in that direction with the rein. I feel that puts the horse on his front end too much; I want his weight shifted more toward the rear, even in circles. What I do is pull my inside hand straight back to my hip. Another advantage of this method: it more closely resembles how you will turn the horse later on with just one hand on the reins. On a finished horse, you should have complete control without moving your hand more than six inches from the horn.

Another mistake is allowing the colt to string out in his lope. Keep him gathered up and collected. And remember that even when he is flexed nicely at the poll, he may not necessarily be collected. A horse can be flexed, yet "strung out behind." To collect a horse, I'll drive his hindquarters under him by slapping him down the outside hind leg with the reins.

"A common mistake is teaching a colt to neck rein too soon."

Expensive Hobby moving right along in a figure-eight. He's relaxed, yet collected and alert.

10 PICKING UP LEADS

There's something we haven't covered yet that is actually simple to do, but very important: picking up the correct lead. Most experienced horsemen have no trouble with this and seldom even think about it. It's just second nature for us to set up the horse to pick up the lead we want, and we begin doing it a little bit when we first start riding the colt outside. But now it's time to get serious and refine our signals so the colt learns to instantly pick up whichever lead we ask for.

Leg pressure is a key part of this, and we've already put some leg on the colt by side-passing and two-tracking him.

You can work on leads outside, but it's easier in the arena, alongside the fence. And let's use the right lead for our example, since most horses have more trouble picking up the right lead than they do the left. I'm not sure why, but most horses have more trouble doing everything to the right. Possibly it's because most of them are "left-handed," whereas most of us are right-handed. Whatever, I know that I usually have to work twice as much doing something to the right with a colt as I do to the left.

To pick up the right lead, walk with the fence on your left, and stay two or three feet away from it. You have two hands on the reins. First, take hold of the horse lightly with both reins. This restrains him slightly, and also elevates his front end a little. Then pull on the left rein a bit more to cock the horse's head to the left—toward the fence. Use the right rein to keep his body from turning left. Apply your left leg just behind the cinch to drive his rear end slightly to the right. Now apply impulsion to make him

break into the canter. Depending on how lazy or active he is, cluck to him, kick him on the left side of the belly, or swat him down the left hind leg with a rein. You always apply impulsion on the outside; when you are moving to the right, apply it on the left side, and vice versa.

Cocking the horse's head to the left and moving his hindquarters to the right puts him at an angle, similar to the angle at which you two-tracked. This angle forces him to take the right lead. Maintaining light contact with the right rein "clears" his right shoulder, keeping it up and making it easy for him to "lead" with that front leg. Applying impulsion on the left side drives his rear end to the right, forcing him to lead with the right hind leg.

To pick up the left lead, do everything just the opposite.

To summarize:

1. Pick up lightly on both reins.
2. Cock head slightly to the fence.
3. Move his rear end toward the inside with your outside leg.
4. Apply impulsion.

Gradually lessen the angle at which you turn the horse until all you have to do is pick up the reins, move them back slightly, touch him with your outside leg, and he immediately picks up the lope on the correct lead. Your cues should become imperceptible...and practice makes perfect.

To make this mare pick up her left lead, I move her a few feet from the fence, and cock her head toward the fence. Note that her front end is elevated slightly.

Now I apply impulsion with my outside leg while keeping my inside leg away from her—and she breaks into a lope on the left lead. I want this mare to move into a left-hand circle, so I'm giving her direction with the inside (left) rein and also applying a little neck rein.

Moving immediately into a circle helps a horse learn to pick up leads more easily...it gives him a reason for doing it.

11 CHANGING LEADS

1. Two photos showing how I ask a finished horse to change leads. In this photo, Expensive Hobby has been traveling on his right lead; I'm gathering him up and have straightened his body to ask him to change to the left.

2. I've changed legs; that is, I've moved my left leg away from him, and he has changed to the left lead.

To some horsemen, the flying change of leads is the icing on the cake in their reining program. Because it is an advanced movement, they feel as if they have conquered the world when they master it.

Teaching a horse to do a series of smooth, fluid changes does give one a feeling of accomplishment and satisfaction, but it is not as difficult as some people make it out to be. If you build to it gradually, laying all the groundwork, it can be easier than you think. Assuming, of course, that your horse has the athletic ability to do it, and you have the talent and *feel* to teach it.

My goal is to be able to change leads on a reining horse anywhere, any time. He should do it smoothly and quietly with no tail switching, speeding up, slowing down, bouncing the rider, or diving into his changes. He should change so fluidly that someone watching only the rider can't tell that the horse under him changed leads.

Finished Horse

Before explaining how I teach the change, it may help if I first explain how I ask a finished horse to change leads. Then you can better understand what I am trying to achieve. It makes no difference whether it's a reining horse, western riding horse, or pleasure horse—I change them all the same.

Assume I am circling on the right lead, and we are going to change to the left at a certain point. My horse is in a good, true, rhythmic three-beat lope; he is not four-beating. As we approach that point, I draw up on the reins slightly, by moving my hand back maybe an inch, to increase contact with the mouth.

When I get that contact, I do two things simultaneously: 1) Move my rein hand slightly to the right to hold him in his circle to the right, and 2) put my left leg on him to move him very slightly to the right for two or three strides (it is so slight that an observer doesn't notice it). For those two or three strides, the horse is moving forward in a slight two-track to the right, with his right shoulder somewhat ahead of his rear end. This does what I call "clear the shoulder"; in this case, the left shoulder.

By now I'm at the point where I want to ask the horse to change. Again, I do two things simultaneously: 1) Move my hand back to center, and pull a little bit more to steady the front end, and 2) move my left leg away from the horse. When the leg pressure is released on his left side, his hip will follow my leg, and when it does, he changes leads.

To change from the left lead to the right, I do everything just the opposite.

My method for changing leads is a little different from the way many people do it; i.e., cueing the horse to change by booting or applying pressure from the outside leg. My horses change when I release pressure from my inside leg. Although the other method works fine for many people, I feel that I can get smoother, prettier, and fancier changes with my method.

I do not neck-rein to cue the horse to change leads, although moving my hand back to center (over the saddle horn) is somewhat of a cue. But my rein hand primarily steadies the front end so the horse does not drop his inside shoulder and dive into his change. My horses, when they are completely trained, change leads, both front and behind, off my leg cue.

1. Another sequence of photos showing Hobby changing leads. Here, he's relaxed while loping on the right lead.

2. We're coming through the center of our figure-eight. I'm collecting Hobby, and holding him over slightly to the right, although we're moving on a straight line.

"The ultimate is changing both leads simultaneously."

3. I continue to hold him in a straight line while I take my left leg off him. In the next stride he will be in the left lead.

4. After changing, Hobby moves in the left-hand circle in a relaxed manner.

On a finished horse, I never apply any outside leg pressure unless he misses the change. For example, if he missed changing from the left to the right, I would put my left leg on him, or maybe even boot him, and also pull back a bit more with my rein hand.

I do not shift my body weight as a cue to change leads. I feel this throws the horse off balance, and possibly shifts more of his weight to his front end, which lets his hindquarters slide out of the circle, causing him to miss the hind-lead change. It's better to sit still and keep your weight in one place.

When my horse changes, I want his backbone straight because he can't change efficiently or smoothly if he has a bend in his body. I also want him to change leads in front and behind simultaneously. A front change first is dead wrong because that means the horse is dropping his shoulder. A hind change first is better, but the ultimate is changing both leads simultaneously.

Another very important point is the rider's feeling of what the horse is doing under him. Some people, no matter how many times they read this book, aren't going to be able to get their horses trained correctly unless they learn to feel what their mounts are doing.

When it comes to changing leads, I feel for the motion to be right, and for the down stride of the front feet. That is, I ask the horse to change when I feel his front feet going down and touching the ground. Then when they come up, he'll

69

"I NEVER drop to the trot to pick up the new lead."

change. If I wait until his feet are coming up, they've got to come all the way up, go back down, and then come up and change.

It's easy to feel where the feet are on a pleasure horse traveling at a slow lope, but you can also feel it on a reining horse moving at a faster speed.

Okay. That's how I ask a finished horse to change. Now let's talk about how we accomplish that.

Young Horse

After a colt can pick up his leads, has learned to two-track and side-pass, and is loping circles well on our desert rides, I want to find out if he has any talent for changing leads naturally. There are three tests I use that help me evaluate the colt, and I do them in the arena where I have a fence to help me.

In the first test, assume I'm loping big circles on the right lead in the middle of the arena, well away from the fence. After a few circles, I straighten the colt out and aim him right at the fence (see diagram No. 1). When we are five or six strides from the fence, his weight will start shifting because he doesn't know

what he's supposed to do. Sometimes he will change on his own; if he doesn't I'll change my reins and let him break off to the left. That is, I pull his nose slightly to the left, apply the right rein against his neck, and my right leg against his side. If he's got any agility at all, he'll change leads and go on. This tells me that the colt has a lot of natural ability.

In another test (diagram No. 2), I bring him into the fence at more of an angle. When he's a couple of strides from the fence, I'll ask him to change. This angle sets him up in a good position to change, with a little help from me. If he changes easily, it tells me that he will probably be a pretty good lead-changer.

In a third test (diagram No. 3), the colt is almost forced to change leads. I bring him into the fence at about a 45-degree angle, and then almost roll him back to make him change. Sometimes this test will "awaken" a colt as to what he's supposed to do, and he'll go on to become a fair lead-changer.

One thing I NEVER do in teaching a colt to change is drop to the trot to pick up the new lead. All that teaches him is to make what I call a lazy lead change. If you always drop to the trot to change,

Traveling on the right lead, this mare is collected and ready to change leads.

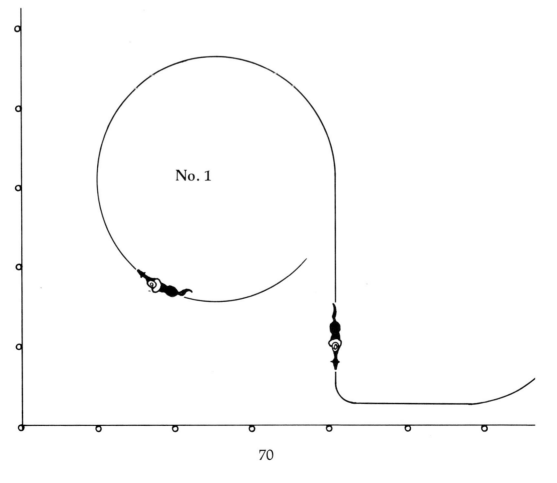

No. 1

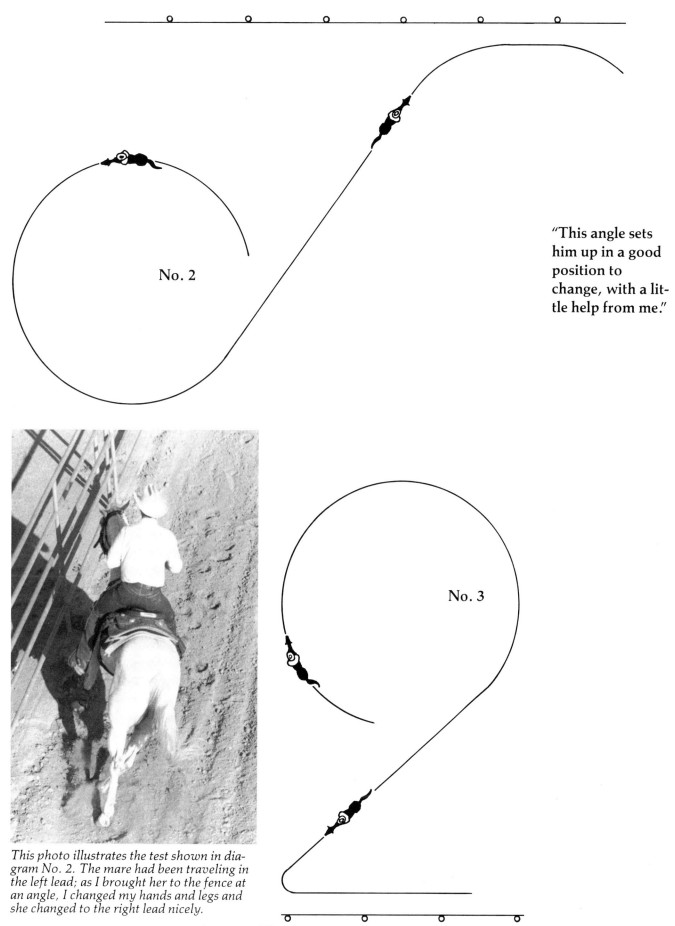

No. 2

"This angle sets him up in a good position to change, with a little help from me."

No. 3

This photo illustrates the test shown in diagram No. 2. The mare had been traveling in the left lead; as I brought her to the fence at an angle, I changed my hands and legs and she changed to the right lead nicely.

71

Loping a big circle on the left lead in the 66 drill. From here, I'll straighten the mare out and head diagonally across the arena to the far corner.

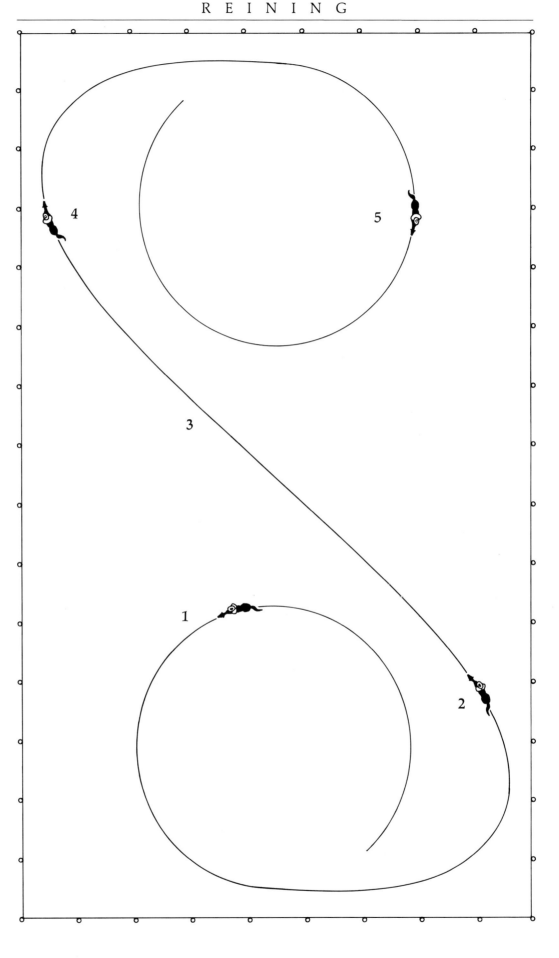

66 Drill

1) Make one or more large, round circles on left lead. 2) Head diagonally across arena. 3) Continue loping on left lead. 4) Change to right lead. 5) Make one or more large round circles on right lead, and repeat drill going the other way.

72

pretty soon that's all the colt wants to do.

Now that I have a good idea of the colt's ability to change leads, we can go into all kinds of drills, and one of my favorites is what I call the 66 drill. Here's how you do it. At one end of the arena, you make a circle, or several circles, with the colt under control and with you rating his speed. You should be moving at a controlled hand-gallop.

After making several circles, head diagonally across the length of the arena to the far end. Let's say you were circling on the left lead at the south end. Now you head to the northwest corner, on the left lead, and at a hand gallop. Your right rein and right leg are against the colt to hold him in the left lead. Aim for a spot on the fence about ten feet from the corner. When you are about ten feet from the fence (see diagram), remove your right leg and apply your left leg to drive his hip under him. At the same time, put your left rein against his neck, as you check back slightly with both reins. He will change leads, and now you make several circles to the right at this end of the arena; then repeat the drill going back the other way.

Aiming the colt at a spot about ten feet from the corner still puts some force on him to change leads, but not as much as before. The corner gives him more room to change on his own. By this time, he's beginning to associate that when he approaches a fence, he's got to jump his hip up under him and change leads—and that he changes when I change legs on him.

Remember when I mentioned in the chapter on "Circles" that I like to stop a colt and roll-back to the inside? I explained that kept him on his inside hock and was a "building block" in learning to change leads later. Well, this is where that training begins to pay off. The colt has learned to turn with his inside hock under him...and that's just what I'm asking him to do in these tests. Because of the previous work, it is easier for him to change when I work him off the fence.

The 66 drill also lays the groundwork for my eventual goal: that he changes when I move my leg away from him. After he's accomplished this drill, I'm ready to start changing him as we gallop across the center of the arena. When we reach the point where I want to change, I just change my legs and hands, and he should change leads on the straightaway.

When I change hands, I also check back a little because I want the horse to stay fairly much at the same speed when he changes; I don't want him developing the habit of charging off when he changes. When a colt wants to do this, I'll forget changing leads for awhile and lope more circles until he learns to stay at the same speed.

When this colt has reached the point where he can change leads in the wide, open spaces—meaning either the middle of the arena or out in the desert or field—I start to put a more formal lead change on him in the circle drill.

Let's assume I'm in the middle of the desert or arena, well away from any fence, and loping on the right lead. After I've loped a circle, or several circles, I come to a complete stop, side-pass to the right about six feet, then change hands and legs and lope off on the left lead, straight ahead. This forms the basis for everything I will do when I make the flying change of leads. In other words, the horse should make a nice, round circle, have the ability to two-track slightly into the center of the circle, or stay straight (straight is optimum), and then when I change hands and legs, he should change leads and lope off in a straight line.

When I "change hands," that means I'll pull back slightly, then touch him lightly on the neck with the right rein and hold his front end steady with the left rein. When I "change legs," I remove my left leg and apply my right leg just behind the front cinch. When circling to the left and changing to the right, I do everything just the opposite.

You may be wondering what this drill accomplishes that simply stopping and then picking up the lope on the other lead doesn't accomplish. When the horse learns this drill, you can make him change leads at any place, any time, simply by checking him back slightly with the reins, holding him over with your outside leg, and then changing him.

If you stop, and then pick up the other lead, the horse hasn't learned to respond to any leg pressure or release (from leg pressure). The same is true with the drop-to-the-trot change of leads. Be-

After changing to the right lead in the 66 drill, I'll lope a couple of big circles, then head diagonally across the arena again.

sides, as I already mentioned, that teaches him to make a lazy lead change, and also causes his back to become concave rather than convex.

This drill also teaches the horse to keep his body straight when he changes, and not to dive into his circles.

After doing this circle drill for maybe two weeks, the horse will become so accustomed to it that when you come to the center of the arena and pull up on the reins, he will stop; as soon as you apply your outside leg, he will side-pass, and when you change legs, he will lope off in a straight line without dropping his hip or shoulder, and move into the other circle. Now we're ready for changing leads in a figure-8.

I like to make two round circles, each about 100 feet in diameter for right now.

In the circle drill, I make several circles in the same direction, then stop.

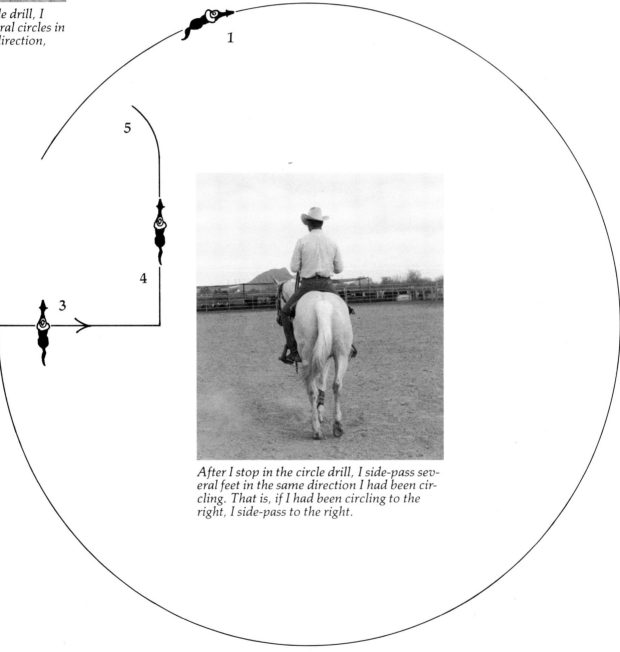

After I stop in the circle drill, I side-pass several feet in the same direction I had been circling. That is, if I had been circling to the right, I side-pass to the right.

Circle Drill

1) Make large round circle. 2) Stop. 3) Side-pass. 4)Pick up new lead and continue moving in straight line for several strides. 5) Move into new circle.

1. A sequence of six photos illustrating the circle drill. We've been loping a left-hand circle, and are moving onto the straight line between circles.

2. Stopping on the straight line between two imaginary circles.

3. Side-passing to the left.

4. After side-passing several feet, I adjust my hands and legs to ask for the right lead.

5. I'm adding impulsion as the mare breaks into the right lead. She's still moving straight ahead.

6. Now we begin circling to the right to continue the drill.

"I like to change leads on a straight line."

As the diagram shows, the two circles should connect in the center on a straight line.

I like to change leads on this straight line. Assume I'm loping on the right lead. As we move onto the imaginary straight line, I'm going to apply my left leg and left rein and two-track to the right for several strides. This "clears his left shoulder" so he does not lean toward the left, causing him to duck his shoulder to the left and miss his hind lead. Then when I want him to change, I simultaneously move my left leg away, apply even pressure with both reins, and put my right leg on him. The horse will change leads while staying in a straight line; then we move off into the other circle. I do not apply any rein pressure on the right side of his neck; that would push him into the left circle, and I want him to keep moving straight for several more strides.

You can do all sorts of things in this

Moving on to the straight line between two imaginary circles where I would ask him to change leads.

Expensive Hobby traveling correctly while making a pretty circle.

figure-8 drill. Normally, I two-track the horse about two feet into the center of the circle. But if he is anticipating the change, I might two-track him farther. Or I might drop my left leg off and continue in a right-hand circle. Or keep my left leg on him and go ahead and change directions, but keep the horse on a counter-canter, or false lead. Or stop and back up. Or whatever is necessary to keep the horse in a fully controlled figure-8, and until he learns to keep his body straight while he changes.

As the horse progresses in this drill over a period of several months, he gradually learns to change when I check him back lightly with the reins, and simply move my outside leg away from him. I will no longer have to use my other leg. This is what results in smooth, pretty changes.

Traveling on the right lead in a big, round circle.

"For smooth, fluid lead changes, I like to make round circles that connect in the center on a straight line."

12 STOPS

Introduction

"To experience the sliding stop on a good horse is like sitting astride a package of power-packed energy."

A hush falls over the audience as the horse and rider close up their last figure-eight, then ease to a walk as they move toward one end of the arena. The horse walks briskly because he is eager and knows what's next, yet he remains obedient to the reins. The rider glances toward the opposite end, checking for the spot he has already picked out to begin his stop.

He eases the horse into a lope. Smoothly, efficiently, like a well-tuned racing engine, the horse gains momentum with each stride. His hindquarters are driving, his forehand is slightly elevated, and he balances himself on the bridle reins, but does not fight them.

The rider has rated the horse so he achieves peak speed just as he reaches the predetermined spot. Instantly, the rider gives the horse imperceptible slack, then says whoa in a firm voice, sits down in the saddle, and pulls back lightly on the reins.

As if he were built with a hinge in his loins, the horse folds his hindquarters under him, melting into the ground. The momentum from his speed, and the power from his hindquarters, carry him in a spectacular slide. All the while his front feet walk along, not jamming or propping, and his head stays in a natural position. The rider, sitting deep in the saddle, keeps a light hold on the reins. Trailing behind is a set of perfectly aligned tracks, the "11" so coveted by reiners. When the horse reaches the end of the slide, he gathers himself up and waits expectantly for the next signal.

That's the way I like to make my run-down and ask for a stop, and that's the way I'd describe a perfect stop. It's

smooth and spectacular, and to experience it on a good horse is like sitting astride a package of power-packed energy. When a horse bends his back to get in the ground, and has the muscle and power to hold the ground and slide while under full control, it's an experience like no other.

How far you should slide depends a great deal on the ground, but I'd say that 20 to 25 feet is pretty good for most stops. Longer slides are fancier, but not as practical. Traditionally, the hard stop was devised to be able to control cattle; if you were to slide 30 feet beyond the cow in a cowhorse class, you would bomb right by her and she'd get away from you. But I'm not opposed to longer stops, and with a horse that's strictly a reiner, I let him slide to his heart's content.

If the ground's slick and you're running hard, you might go farther than you planned. The longest slide I've made was about 45 feet on hard, pebbly ground with a horse named Bar Thunder. The longest slide I made with Expensive Hobby was 35 feet.

Because the slide is so spectacular, most judges put more emphasis on it than other parts of the pattern. Obviously you must be able to change leads and turn around, but you could have a rough spot there and still win or place high if you make great stops. Or if the rest of your pattern is good and your stops are sensational, you're gonna beat 'em. Judges go for the big stop.

There are actually two ways a horse can stop: 1) he can straighten his stifles and skate along, more or less in a standing-up position, or 2) he can break in the loin and drive his hindquarters under him. Personally, I think the latter is the

"Because the slide is so spectacular, most judges put more emphasis on it than other parts of the pattern."

Dirt boils up as Expensive Hobby breaks in the loin and drives into the ground. He's giving to the bridle nicely, and I'm down on his back and sitting quietly. This is an outstanding stopping picture.

"The real true-blue stopper should be able to stop in any kind of ground."

only way for a versatile horse to stop.

The horse that locks his stifles and skates can look sensational, but he can generally only stop on hard ground that's a little loose on top. In the Midwest and East where this type of stop is more popular, the arena footing is often specially prepared for the reining horses.

But to me, the real true-blue stopper should be able to stop in any kind of ground you put under him—slick and hard, or deep and heavy. And the horse that's built right and has been trained to break in the loin and shove his rear under himself can stop in any ground. He can also get in the ground deep enough to hold his stop. Because this horse is

comfortable when he stops, and has good balance while he's stopping, you can put any kind of ground under him and it won't make any difference to him.

I'm so confident of my horses' ability to stop that I know I can pull a little bit harder and get 'em in the ground when it's deep, like at Reno (Snaffle Bit Futurity); or I can take them back East to the Congress where the ground is harder, and pull a little bit lighter and slide.

But as I mentioned, a horse must be built right to stop this way. He's got to be stout through the loin, powerful in the hindquarters, and have good muscling in the gaskin, especially inside. Then I can train him to stop the way I like.

1. This is a full sequence of Hobby running and stopping, and then relaxing. Here, he's starting to build speed, he's elevated, yet he's under total control. I could ask him to stop right now and he would.

2. A great picture of Hobby running. I'm sitting straight up, but slightly behind the motion, and I'm sitting still so I don't hamper him in any way.

3. He's driven into the ground, and stayed mobile in front. A horse can't get much deeper in the ground than Hobby is here. I'm staying close to his back, although he's pushing hard into the slide. His head is in good position, even though I have a hair more restraint on him than I should.

4. A near-perfect stopping picture, with Hobby's head in ideal position, yielding to the bridle.

5. The end of the slide. Hobby is relaxed, and waiting for my next cue.

Teaching the Stop

After I've been riding a colt about 90 days, I've got him pretty well under control, can rate his speed, and he has the general idea that whoa means stop. Now I want to find out if he can break in the loin and really get in the ground to make reining horse stops.

I already have a pretty good idea if he can because of the way he backs up. The correct backing position is very much like the correct stopping position. To back, the horse must bend his back, shove his rear legs under him, and move in reverse gear fluidly and swiftly. If he can do that, he can probably stick his tail in the ground.

My cues to ask a colt to stop differ slightly from the way I ask a finished horse to stop. For now, I say whoa, sit down in the saddle, then pick up the reins—in that sequence. The first two cues give the colt a chance to begin stopping before I ever take hold of him. As soon as he comes to a complete stop, I release the reins.

This is the same theory as Pavlov's technique with dogs of rewarding them for doing what he asked. I believe you always have to give the horse "someplace to go." Which is to say that if he does something correctly, he gets relief. If you put your leg on him to move him over and he moves, you remove your leg. If you pull on the bridle and he

stops, you drop the reins. And so on. But if you contain the horse and keep asking him when he's already doing what you want, he will get confused and not learn anything.

Usually I start working on the stop while trotting big circles. You have more control of the colt at a trot than at a lope, and the fundamentals for stopping are the same. You could do it at a walk except that the colt won't have enough impulsion to get his hocks under him the way I want.

From the trot, I'll say whoa, sit down, and pull back lightly. I pull one rein a bit more than the other to keep him flexible in front; pulling both reins equally tends to make a horse stiffen up and jam his front legs into the ground. But I don't see-saw the reins because that will make his head go up. I simply take the slack out and pull.

As soon as he stops, I move my hands forward to relieve the pressure, let him stand quietly maybe 20 seconds, then trot off—and ask him to stop again.

Most good colts will stop with just a light pull. With a colt that doesn't want to stop, or lacks the agility to stop, you must go through training processes to make stopping easy for him. I don't want to pull much harder because I don't want to get in his mouth this early in his development. That would soon make him dread stopping—and not have a good feel to his mouth.

I'll help a colt learn to stop by doubling him. In fact, I double all my colts because it improves their lateral flexibility, but I don't double the good colts as hard as the others. Doubling means turning a colt by bending his head and neck sharply. For this work, I double him into the fence. Since the colt is acquainted with fence work from our lead-changing sessions, he has a general idea of what I'm asking him to do.

I move out at a brisk trot, staying about six feet away from the fence (assume it's on my right). When I'm ready, I'll say whoa, sit down, and then immediately double him into the fence by loosening up my outside (left) rein and pulling on the inside rein. I pull him all the way through the turn so we are facing the opposite direction. Without hesitating, I break him off into the trot again, travel about 75 or 100 feet, then

This photo clearly shows the similarity between the backing position and the stop ping position.

"I start working on the stop while trotting big circles."

A perfect "11" is laid down by this palomino mare in a long slide.

1. A series of four photos showing how I double a horse on the fence. This mare is far enough along in her training that I'm loping her instead of trotting. She's on the left lead, and I have her several feet from the fence.

2. As she starts to stop, I pull her into the fence with the right rein, and put a lot of slack in the left rein. She's got her hindquarters under her well and is about to plant her pivot foot.

3. At this point, I'm not applying any impulsion with my outside leg because the mare is coming around nicely.

4. I give her a lot of slack as I break her off in a lope going the other way. She's really driving with her hindquarters.

"No matter how fast a horse may be galloping, you stop him with finesse, not strength."

repeat the drill, this time doubling him to the left. To get impulsion in the turn, I use my outside leg in his side.

Doubling accomplishes several things:

1) Since it slows his forward motion, he learns to begin stopping when he hears "whoa."

2) It makes him learn to use his loin and to drive his hindquarters under him.

3) He learns to get his inside hock under him when I pull on the inside rein. If I'm going to double him to the right and pull on the right rein, he drives his right hock under him so that leg can be the pivotal leg.

4) It keeps his front end flexible. Instead of jamming his front feet into the ground, he learns to use them to help push himself around.

Suppose you have a colt that is belligerent or awkward. When you try to double him, his shoulder keeps going straight ahead even though you have his head pulled toward the fence. What to do? You apply pressure on the outside. If you're trying to double him to the right, you either drive him with your left leg or smack him down the left rear leg with a bridle rein. This will drive him into the fence, making him a believer that he has to follow his nose in the direction it's being pulled.

After a colt has been doubled into the fence a few times each way, he will start checking on his own when I say whoa, if he has any brains at all. I will continue to double him, but will move him a little farther away from the fence so I don't have to pull him quite as hard or bend his neck as far. At the same time, I can still get the drive or power from his hindquarters.

I continue this for several more days, then I'm going to fool him. I'll trot down the fence (assume it's on my right), say whoa, and sit down. He expects to be doubled to the right, so he plants his right rear leg under him. But I out-think him by pulling the left rein harder than the right. Expecting to be pulled to the left, he also brings his left rear leg under him. Now I've got both hind legs under him, and a pretty nice stop. If he has done it well, I let him stand a few moments and pat him on the neck.

Then I try it again. From where he's standing, I turn him into the fence and break him off into a trot. When he's re-

laxed and moving fluidly (not anticipating), again I say whoa and sit down. Thinking that he's going to be doubled to the left, he brings the left leg under him; but I pull harder on the right rein, bringing that leg under him, too. Again, he should make a nice stop. I let him stand, pat him, then trot off and do something else for a while.

If your horse still isn't paying attention to the bridle after this drill, or he's not getting his hocks under him like he should, forget asking him to stop and work on improving his back-up. As I mentioned at the beginning of this chapter, the stopping position is almost the same as the backing position, and you can improve the stop by working on the back-up.

When you pick up the reins to ask the horse to stop, or back up, his body should fold like an accordian. His head should come to the bridle, and his rear end should come to his head. Refer to the chapter on backing. Try to improve your horse's agility and flexibility so he can flow backwards. A horse that backs stiffly will never be able to "glide into the ground." He will be stiff and rigid. We want him to be able to gallop at full speed, then just melt into the ground. Depending on the particular horse, you may have to work on backing him for several weeks, but it's well worth the time, and the best way to improve his stopping ability.

With the good colt that quickly learns to stop well when he's doubled from the trot, I begin asking him to stop from the lope. I use the same procedure, and will even double him into the fence from the lope.

When it becomes firmly fixed in the colt's mind that he folds into the ground when I give him the three cues, I begin increasing the length of his stops by speeding up. More speed gives more momentum for sliding farther. At this stage, I use the same three cues; I do not pull harder just because we are going faster. No matter how fast a horse may be galloping, you stop him with finesse, not strength.

By now, I've probably been riding the colt approximately six months. If he's a good colt, he's stopping well from speed, say a hand gallop. Now I will add a preliminary signal to my sequence of cues.

A good picture showing how I like a horse to break in the loin and melt into the ground.

When a horse is galloping correctly, he is, in effect, running uphill—and this photo illustrates it.

"I keep just enough pressure on the reins to hold the horse in his stop."

Before I say whoa, I move my rein hand forward a couple of inches, for just one or two strides. Next, I will say whoa and sit down simultaneously, then pull back. Here's the reasoning for releasing the bridle reins for a split second:

When a reining horse is galloping correctly, he is, in effect, running uphill. His head stays in the correct position, his front end is elevated, and his hindquarters are driving. If you were to ask him to stop when he's running like this— when he's in midair with his legs fully extended—he would go into the ground too abruptly. He won't be able to slide like he should, and he'll probably bounce a time or two.

What you must do is allow the horse to level out his front end and shorten his stride just a hair. I accomplish that by moving my rein hand forward and dropping the chin strap off the horse. Then when I say whoa and sit down, it's much easier for the horse to get into what we call a "soft start." That means he just melts into the ground.

On a finished reining horse, as soon as I drop him off the bridle, he'll level out and start getting his hindquarters under him. As I sit down and say whoa, he'll begin stopping before I ever pick up on the reins.

On a horse that's burning down the arena, this sequence of cues happens so fast they become almost simultaneous. From the time I move my hand forward until the horse begins stopping, he has probably taken only two strides. As he is stopping, I sit as steadily as I possibly can—keeping my legs quiet and my seat in the saddle. And I keep just enough pressure on the reins to hold the horse in the stop.

One thing I should clarify is the term "sit down in the saddle" when I ask the horse to stop. This doesn't mean I've been standing in the stirrups beforehand. Instead, it refers to a redistribution of my weight. When I'm galloping a reining horse, I am sitting down—but only about 60% of my weight is in the saddle. The other 40% is in my stirrups. When I ask the horse to stop, I round my back slightly and roll my hips under me so about 75% of my weight is now in the saddle.

Some reining horse riders like to get their weight off the horse's loin, believ-

ing this makes it easier for the horse to get his hindquarters under him. Whether a rider sits down or gets his weight off the loin, I think the most important thing is to stay as quiet and as balanced as you can. It's tough for a horse to stop correctly if the rider's weight is shifting over his back.

Problems

Let's say this horse is stopping pretty good, but then he develops a problem. Suppose I am moving at a brisk lope, I drop off the bridle just a hair, say whoa and sit down, then start to pull. The horse gets into the ground a little bit, but doesn't stop completely. What to do?

I'll probably double him. I'll lope him out, ask him to stop, then take one rein and pull his front end around so he has to drive his inside back leg under him. As soon as he comes around, I'll set him down to stop his forward motion, then back him up. What this does is accentuate my "request" for him to stop; he knows that he will be reprimanded.

The next time I lope him down the arena and say whoa, he's going to be thinking harder about how to get into the stop. But if he doesn't stop, I'll double him the other way, which will "even up his sides." Generally this is all that's necessary to get a good horse stopping correctly again.

Sometimes you have to analyze in what part of the stop a problem is occurring…the beginning, the middle, or maybe he's walking out of it at the end. If it's at the beginning, you might need to pull the horse a little harder initially, then ease up on the bridle reins and let him go ahead and glide.

If he's walking out of the stop at the end, then you need to take an extra hold of him toward the end of his slide to keep him in the ground.

If he's not getting any distance to his slides, the solution is to add speed, keep him relaxed, and keep his hocks pushing evenly. Leave his head as loose as you can so that he can slide and stay relaxed. Then he'll walk along in front instead of jamming his front feet into the ground. Maintain just enough rein contact to keep the horse balanced. If you overpull, you're going to get him too far on his hocks, and then he won't get any dis-

*This gray mare has
the ability to stop
hard and stay mobile
in front, but she is
stiff in the poll and
needs too much pull.
She needs considera-
ble work to soften the
poll before I ask her
for any more hard
stops, and I can do
that with either the
hackamore or snaffle.*

tance at all.

Sometimes I must vary from my sequence of cues in stopping a horse. Take,
for example, a horse that is low-necked,
or that runs downhill. I will continue to
drive him and lift the reins to elevate his
front end all the way through the run.
When I reach the point of the stop, I will
merely sit down and say whoa, and continue to keep tension on the reins. This
keeps him balanced properly so he can
get his rear end under him to sit down
and slide.

As you and your horse get the hang of
stopping, you will develop a feel for how
much you need to pull him. Most of the
time, the horse will tell you how much to
pull. This means that after you have re-

leased the bridle as the first cue, then
picked up the reins again and are holding
the reins steady, the horse will take hold
of the bit to balance himself while he
slides.

You NEVER overpower the horse to
stop him. If you go flying down the
arena and then rip his head off, he'll start
scotching badly, or will dive into his stop
to brace himself and protect his mouth.

Which brings us to the subject of bits.
I'm a devout believer that if you cannot
get a horse to stop in the snaffle, you're
probably not going to get him to stop
well in anything. If you have to use force
to make him stop, he will never be any
great shakes as a reining horse.

To be a great stopper, a horse must

1. Four overhead shots showing a three-year-old mare running and stopping. Here, she's in a good, relaxed gallop.

2. A split second before I ask her to stop, I'm concentrating on sitting quietly in the correct position.

"To be a great stopper, a horse must want to stop."

3. I've given her the initial cue of "whoa," and now I'm staying down on her back and keeping my hands light. Some horses stop so hard that even a good rider is momentarily left in mid-air when the hindquarters drop out from under him. This mare looks stiff in the front end because when a horse is first asked to stop, he reaches for the bridle and puts one or both front feet on the ground.

As the mare gets into the stop, she becomes more flexible with her front legs which will allow her to slide farther. She's giving nicely to the bridle, and I've settled into the saddle.

want to stop. That's why a reining horse must have a super mind.

Once a horse stops well in the snaffle, you've got to find a bit he is comfortable with when you show him. Horses vary in their preferences; some like a bit with more weight, or a higher port, or a lower port, or more leverage. Sometimes when we put more bridle (a bit with more leverage) on a horse, he can balance himself better in the stop. Or the opposite can be true. Sometimes we have too much bridle on a horse and we need to back off. A case in point is the horse that wants to raise his head too much in the stop. We shouldn't put more bridle on him to "hold his nose down"; we should try to relax him by using a milder bit on him.

Sometimes you have to go through quite a number of bits before you find one the horse likes best, and that's why most trainers have so many bits hanging in their tack rooms.

Whether I use a curb chain or curb strap depends on the horse. If he's light-mouthed and responsive, there's nothing nicer to show him in than a flat leather curb strap because you get a better feel of the horse with leather than you do with a chain. And when a horse is exceptionally light and I want to take a little more hold of the bridle (bit), I may have to use a curb strap because a chain might keep him off the bridle too much (scare him).

But I'm not adverse to using a curb chain. I'm not out to impress anybody by riding with a curb strap, especially if they are using a curb chain and beat me. If a curb chain will increase the lightness and responsiveness of a horse without scaring him, I'll use it. When a horse is not responding well to a mild bit and leather curb, I think it's better to put more bridle and a curb chain on him rather than pulling him harder.

1. Three sequence pictures of Expensive Hobby stopping. Here, I've already given him a little slack to release the curb strap, as I do on a finished horse. I've said whoa and sat down. He has reached for the bridle and taken the slack out of the reins, and is gathering himself together. I haven't started to pull yet.

2. This is the initial stage of the stop. He's driving into the ground, but staying mobile in front. Note the position of his head; he's relaxed in the bridle, and is not over-flexed. I'm pulling him only as hard as it takes to keep him balanced in the stop, and I'm sitting down in the saddle.

3. He's gotten deeper into the ground here, but continues to stay elevated and flexible in front. If you will check his head position in all three pictures, it has hardly changed at all—an outstanding feat for this kind of hard run and stop.

The Run-Down

The run-down deserves attention because, in my opinion, the stop is an extension of the run, and the run is all-important in how well the horse stops. If the horse isn't running correctly, he can't stop correctly.

During the run-down, you need full control of the horse so you can rate his speed, and he must run in a straight line. I'll start this with a colt by trotting him from one end of the arena to the other—all the way into the fence (it's called "fencing the horse"). If he begins to drift off, say to the right, I'll bring him back on course with the left rein. Later when he's farther along in his training, he will know to stay between the reins. If he drifts, I can straighten him up with a neck rein.

When the colt has trotted all the way to the fence, I say whoa and sit down, but don't pull. I let him stop by himself while I concentrate on keeping him straight. I don't want him to develop the habit of veering off. I want him to go straight into the fence. When he will trot

nicely down the arena in a straight line, I begin loping him.

I keep him at a slow lope; again my primary goal is teaching him to lope down the arena in a straight line. Obviously, if a horse is drifting or leaning from one side to the other when he's run-

1. A sequence of four photos illustrating how I "fence" a horse. I start this with a colt by trotting him, but I'm letting this mare gallop because she's well along in her training. Here, I'm concentrating on keeping her running straight.

2. I'm staying close to her back to steady her as she goes to the fence.

3. As she approaches the fence, I say whoa, and concentrate on staying down in the saddle and keeping my hands steady to keep her straight. She's starting to stop, although I'm not pulling on her.

4. I allow the fence to stop the mare. I'm pulling lightly— mostly to steady the mare and keep her straight. Over-pulling would defeat the reason for fencing her.

"Once the horse knows how to stop well, I don't do it very often."

ning, he can't stop as straight or get the distance in his slide that he can when he's running straight.

When he's a few strides from the fence, I say whoa and sit down, and let him stop by himself.

The next step is to teach him to rate his speed. I always want to start slowly, and with a green horse, I might even let him trot a few strides before breaking into a lope. Then each stride he takes down the arena should be a little bit faster so he reaches his peak speed at the end of his run. You want the horse running uphill into his stop. You cannot get a fabulous stop from a horse running downhill since his weight is more on his front end than his hindquarters.

We don't want the horse to break into a dead run immediately because then he has no way to build speed. And NEVER do we want the horse to start slow and remain slow all the way to the center of the arena, and then give a sudden burst of speed just before he stops. That will result in the horse learning to back off when speed is asked for, leveling out too soon, or scotching.

It also reveals that the horse might not be willing to run the length of the arena. If the rider does this time after time, the horse will get smarter and smarter. He knows that when the rider guns him, the

A good, deep stop on a three-year-old mare.

stop is next, and the horse may decide to skip the speed and stop now.

There is one exception to starting slowly and building speed gradually, and that's when you are supposed to stop in the middle of the arena. Then you let the horse break and run a little bit freer, but you still keep his front end elevated.

While the horse is making his run-down, I keep light contact with the reins to rate his speed. Just as you never see a race horse running with a lot of slack in the reins, you'll never see a good reining horse running with slack. He needs the bridle for balance, and you need to keep contact so you can rate his speed, and so you can elevate his front end as he runs.

He should start his run-down with a lot of control, and each stride should be a little bit faster until you attain the *maximum speed you want.* I say that because you don't want some horses to run wide open—those that can't control their stop as well as they can when they are rated back just a little.

When you reach that maximum speed, that's when you should stop. The horse will be slightly elevated and running uphill into the stop, and his momentum will carry him forward into a slide. If he were slowing down, it would be more difficult for him to get his hindquarters under him.

Every time I make a run-down, I want the horse to think he's going all the way to the fence. I don't want him to think he's stopping when he's 40 feet from the fence. If he starts checking, he will not have the kind of motion going into the ground that he needs to make a beautiful stop. Therefore I will occasionally "fence" a finished horse, meaning I will gallop him right to the fence.

However, I am careful about how I do this, because I'm an advocate of a horse wanting to run to the fence. He certainly won't if he's punished and driven into the fence hard, time after time. Here's how I do it: About 20 feet from the fence, I'll drop some slack into the bridle reins, say whoa, and steer him to keep him straight. I let him go into the fence anyway he wants to.

That makes him get his hindquarters under him, which saves some work on my part. Plus I think he enjoys it. But he won't if he's driven into the fence harder, and harder, and harder. Finally it will be difficult to get him anywhere close to the fence.

Once a horse understands that he runs from "fence to fence," you don't have to do it very often. In fact, you shouldn't. If you need to work on stops, you can do it without fencing him. You can lope your horse around the arena, just off the rail, build speed gradually, and then while he's on the straightaway, ask him to stop.

Some of the good reining horse trainers in the Midwest and East have mini-racetracks in their pastures or fields, with the footing carefully prepared to facilitate sliding. These tracks have no fencing.

You can teach a horse to rate his speed out in the field or desert better than you can in the arena. Once again...in the arena, the horse is thinking barn, or gate, or other horses. Out in a wide open area, there are no distractions. I can let a horse run hard for maybe 300 feet, then pick him up and lope for another 300 feet, then gain speed again. Once you have the control to rate a horse out in the open, it's a great advantage when you take him in the arena.

In my case, I have places out in the desert where I'll ask a horse to stop. They are level areas with good footing.

Once a horse knows how to stop, and can stop well, I don't do it very often. It simply isn't necessary when a horse is broke; continuing to do it will take some of the sparkle and style out of his stop. When I was showing Expensive Hobby in reining and cowhorse classes, rarely did I ever stop him hard except in a class. I knew him so well, and had so much faith in him, that I knew he'd stop the best he could whenever I asked him.

1. A sequence of seven photos showing Expensive Hobby making another good run-down and stop. I let him build speed more quickly this time because I want more room at the other end of the arena to make a longer slide. As we break into the lope, he's driving off his hindquarters.

2. We are about half-way through our run at this point. He's still driving off his hind-quarters and running uphill, and is in full stride. I have contact on the bridle; this is what we call "running on the bridle." I'm urging him to run uphill into the bridle.

3. I've released the bridle to give him a little slack so he can level out his front end and shorten his stride just a hair. Notice that his hindquarters are higher than in the previous photograph. What he's going to do now is readjust and gather his hind feet up for the stop.

4. His hocks are still bent just a little as he melts into the ground.

5. He's down in a full stop and sliding.

6. He continues to get deeper into the ground. I'm sitting down in the middle of the saddle, trying not to hamper him in any way.

7. He's beginning to recover at the end of the stop.

13 TURN-AROUNDS

"The turn-around should be flat, with no up-and-down motion like a rocking chair."

About the only thing we haven't taught this colt yet is how to turn-around, or spin as it's also called. Actually, I think turn-around is a more accurate description of what the horse is doing: turning around on his hind legs, which serve as the pivot point. When I think of a spin, I think of a top, and a horse doesn't spin like a top does; or at least he shouldn't. A top spins in the middle, and if a horse did that, he'd be swapping ends.

Like other maneuvers in the reining pattern, we start this one slowly, building our foundation. Initially, we only ask for half-turns, but our goal is for this colt to plant his pivot foot and turn around smoothly, with consistency. A good horse turns so fast that the rider can lose track of how many times he has turned. I know. That happened to me on Expensive Hobby, who could turn around faster than any horse I've ridden. Yet he always maintained correct form. Speed is essential in a turn-around, but you've got to have form, too.

The turn-around should be flat, with no up-and-down motion like a rocking chair. That's wasted motion. The horse should plant his inside hind foot as his pivot foot, and practically drill a hole into the ground with it while he turns. The outside hind foot is the driver; it helps push the horse around, and so does the outside front leg. The inside front leg comes off the ground, moves over, and sets down. Overall, the horse gives an impression of flowing around with extreme speed.

That's the way I like a horse to turn around, and I'm not sure what you'd call it. I say this because you often hear people talk about loping turn-arounds and trotting turn-arounds—to describe how

a horse uses his front end. In a loping turn, the horse's front end goes up and down; I don't care for it because the horse loses speed coming off the ground so much. In what's called the trotting turn-around, the front end stays more level while the outside front leg crosses over the inside leg, which is correct form, but it doesn't accurately describe a good, fast, flat turn. When a horse is turning properly with speed, he's darn sure not trotting around, and he's not loping because he's turning so flat. This is vividly shown in the AQHA films titled *Survival of the Fittest* and *The Working Cow Horse*, which have some phenomenal slow-motion footage of Expensive Hobby turning around.

It's spectacular to watch, and if you analyze Hobby's motion, you can see that he's not trotting or loping around. I don't know of any term for how I like a horse to turn—other than FAST and FLAT—but here's how I teach it.

At this stage, "our" colt will follow his nose when I pull the inside rein. He knows how to walk, trot, and lope a circle with his neck, shoulders, rib cage, and rear end all following his nose on the same track. I've rolled him into the fence, and when this happens, he knows to bring his inside hock under him. With just a very light pull on the bridle, he backs up straight and with some dispatch.

I want to emphasize that the colt must be able to walk in a small circle and follow his nose, giving to the rein correctly, like we do when circling bushes in the desert. The colt should be able to make smaller and smaller circles, but not to the degree that he breaks into a full-

1. Here are two great shots of Expensive Hobby, who could really "burn the turns." When I say a horse has got to set his inside pivot foot when he turns, this is what I mean.

2. Hobby is staying low to the ground, has his pivot foot set well, is giving to the rein, and driving hard.

"The colt must learn to make good half turns first."

fledged turn. For that, he's got to be set on his hind end, and I haven't wanted to do that yet, except when he's backing. To set him on his hindquarters and make a correct full turn from a circle, I would have to restrain him so much (with the reins) that it would create resistance in his mouth. I don't want that to happen.

By this time, a lot of good colts have so much feel and ability that it's a great temptation to make a full turn (360 degrees). But you've got to restrain yourself. First grade must always be completed before second grade, and the colt must learn to make good half turns first.

Let's assume I'm going to make a half turn to the right. I gather the colt up and begin backing him, lightly and quickly. When I'm ready to turn, I simply drop pressure off the left rein while I keep contact with the right; I do not pull any harder. This allows his head to come around to the right a little. Since he knows how to follow his head, that, combined with the motion from backing up, automatically results in his body flowing around and over his hocks in a

half turn.

That is the foundation of my turn-around. At this point, I do not use any pressure from my outside rein, but I might apply pressure from my outside leg to make his side follow through. Impulsion should not be necessary because the colt has plenty of motion if he is backing properly. I simply redirect that motion with my inside rein to turn the colt over his hocks.

I like this method because backing puts the colt on his rear end, and isolates the rear end while the front end turns itself. If the colt were simply standing still, or even walking in a small circle, I would have to pull too hard to get him to turn and also isolate the hind end at the same time. Backing the colt sets him on his rear end, and dropping the outside rein lets him flow over himself without my pulling on him, or driving him with impulsion. It's a very simple method. It teaches him to plant his pivot foot and turn freely.

A good colt who is agile and well schooled in the basics can make this half

Being able to flex is a fundamental for learning to turn around correctly.

This mare is giving her head nicely.

Flexing to the left with no resistance.

1. In the learning stages of making a half turn, I gather the filly up and begin backing her.

2. She is backing lightly and freely, and has her hocks under her. To make a half turn to the right, I give her total slack in the left rein and continue pulling with the right.

3. I pull her on through the turn. Ideally, she should make a clean "sweep" with her front feet; that is, they should not touch the ground until the half turn is completed. Note the complete slack in the left rein so it does not hinder her.

4. When she completes the half turn, I give her slack in both reins.

"We drill proper form into him through repetition while he's still in the snaffle."

If a colt lacks agility, I will trot small circles...

...then screw him down into a flat turn-around. I generally do this in a snaffle, but this mare is working nicely in a hackamore.

turn easily. After he can do it well in both directions, the next step is to turn him with a little forward motion. I'll trot him forward in a medium-size circle, then do what I call *set him*. I check back on the reins to stop his movement forward, release pressure on the outside rein, and pull lightly with the inside rein to bring him around in a half-turn. I pause to let him think about what we've done, and trot off again.

With the ideal colt, I am still asking him to turn by only pulling lightly on the inside rein. Checking and setting him puts him on his hocks, and pulling on the inside rein redirects his forward motion into a half turn. Doing this while moving in a circle makes it easier on the colt because it gives him direction.

The colt is ready for the next step when he can:

1) Make these half turns fluidly and easily without much pull on the inside rein.

2) Walk in very small circles following his nose.

3) Back quickly from a very light pull.

The next step is to take the colt through some real small turns, walking slowly and easily. Earlier, I said I didn't want to make a full turn from a circle because the colt didn't know how to plant his rear end yet. But now he does. While

I'm walking him in a small circle, I'll check him back lightly to get him on his rear end, and ask him to turn around. I primarily use the inside rein, but I might use the outside rein for a little stimulus— and because he will eventually turn from the outside rein only.

While he's slowly turning, I'll watch over his inside shoulder to make sure his inside front foot is getting out of the way, and that the outside front foot is crossing over properly.

When he does this well in both directions, it's time to add some forward impulsion so he turns with more speed. I'll pull a little bit more on the inside rein to make the inside shoulder come faster. And I will use a little outside rein and foot to generate more speed, and to make sure the outside of his body is following.

If the colt comprehends most of what you have taught him so far, but lacks agility, take him to a corner in the arena and trot several fast, small circles. Concentrate on increasing his forward motion and getting him to trot around in rhythmic fashion. Once he can do that, use light contact to screw him down into a flatter, more forward-type of turn-around. (Having the fence on two sides will help contain him.) This gets him to thinking *forward* and *around,* which should help make it easier for him to flow around.

Here's something that may help you better comprehend a turn-around. In a turn-around, you point the horse's nose, and the body tries to catch up. The faster the nose goes, the faster the body and legs must come. When you finally put the horse in the bridle and touch him with the outside rein, his nose should still lead while his body and legs try to catch up.

We drill this into him through repetition while he's still in the snaffle. We show him the proper form with repetition. Gradually I use less inside rein and more outside rein to ask him to turn; he knows that his head should always turn first, followed by his neck, shoulders, side, and then he should drive. He should go faster and faster, depending on how much touch you have on the outside of his neck.

Expensive Hobby had so much feel on

his neck that when I touched him with the outside rein, he reacted like it was scalding hot.

You have to be careful not to use too much outside rein too soon. That can cause his head to go too far to the inside, resulting in his body not being straight. It can even cause the head to arc to the outside if the horse hasn't been trained properly to this point and can't follow his nose.

To ask for more speed, use your outside foot as the accelerator, generally right in the area of the back cinch. That drives the rib cage toward your inside hand that you're pulling with. If he's broke properly and knows to follow his nose, the more you push with your foot, the faster he should go.

If he's dragging his outside shoulder, you can encourage it to move faster by using your foot at the elbow or shoulder. But again, use caution. Make sure you have checked him back a little to get his rear end under him. Otherwise, if you go to the shoulder without giving him good direction (meaning he doesn't follow his nose properly), it will cause his rear end to come out of the ground.

If you have followed all these steps carefully and have a talented horse, he will keep his hindquarters planted in the ground, move his front end well, follow his nose, and bring his outside body correctly. And you can go as fast as you want, for as many turns as you want, depending on how much impulsion you use.

> "Expensive Hobby reacted to the rein like it was scalding hot."

1. Expensive Hobby at the beginning of a turn-around to the right.

2. Now he's starting to gain speed. Note how he is driving with his outside (left) feet.

1. *The start of a turn-around to the left. I'm asking more for proper position at this point rather than speed, so I'm only lightly reining him. He's positioning his pivot foot.*

2. *Hobby is starting to gain speed. He's crossing over well in front, and has his pivot foot under his belly where it belongs. This photo also illustrates how you point the horse's nose in a turn-around and the rest of his body tries to catch up. You can also see how my body is twisted slightly to the inside. My inside foot is still, while my outside foot is free to act as the accelerator.*

3. He's gaining more speed and continues to give his head to the inside. The spread of his front feet indicates a lot of agility.

4. Hobby is readjusting his right hind leg so he can drive with it. This photo also shows the slight twist in my body to the inside, and how I'm sitting on my left hip. In all four of these sequence photos, notice that my rein hand has stayed consistent in the pressure I put on his neck. There are times when you have to give and take if the horse sits back too far or moves forward; but in this turnaround, Hobby's form has been so consistent, I have been able to apply consistent pressure.

1. *A sequence of seven photos showing Expensive Hobby turning to the right. Here, he's just giving his head as he starts to the right.*

2. *As he brings his shoulder through, you can see his pivot foot reach under his belly.*

3. *A great shot showing his pivot foot where it belongs, and how he's picking up his inside front foot and crossing over with the outside front foot.*

4. He's gaining a lot of speed. He's just pushed off with his front feet and raised a lot of dirt with them.

5. I've gathered him up just a little with the reins to keep my timing in sync with him. This photo also shows how I look at the inside ear in a turn-around. Looking any farther to the inside throws my timing off. Note how Hobby is crossing over with his outside front foot, and that my rein hand is just a few inches from the saddle horn in the direction we are going. I've got just a light touch on his neck to keep him flowing through the turn-around.

6. I've put a minute amount of slack in the reins to ease off as we approach the end of the turn-around.

7. We are completing the turn-around…he's starting to relax and return to a neutral position.

Problems

Thus far we have assumed we are working with a good colt...one who has no trouble making half turns and can easily makes full turns. But we are not always fortunate enough to have such agile colts, so let's go back and look at some of the problems we can encounter, in making either half turns, full turns, or both.

Here are several that are typical: 1) The colt lacks agility in his front end, and interferes in front, stepping on himself. 2) He backs over his hocks. 3) He doesn't stay on his pivot foot. 4) He lacks impulsion when he comes around.

Here again, the rider must be skilled enough to tell what the problem is, which is why it's so important to be able to feel what the horse is doing under you...so you can tell if his shoulder is dragging, or his rib cage is hanging out, or whatever.

Problem 1—Lacks agility, and interferes in front. By now you should know if the colt is agile by how well he backs, gives his head, circles, etc. If he's really stiff and lacks coordination, you might have to aim him at another event that requires less athletic talent. But if you think he still shows promise for reining, trotting a lot of circles—as we have already explained—will increase his agility for turning around.

Maintain the colt's body in the proper position. Gradually make the circles smaller so the colt learns to cross his outside front foot over the inside...as he must do in a turn-around. Continue decreasing the size of the circles until he anchors his rear end and crosses his outside front leg over the inside leg as he turns. Then move him out and begin trotting larger circles again.

You can also double this colt on the fence, and back him and make half turns until he learns to use his front end correctly. When you ask him for the half turn, applying outside impulsion will drive him around the inside rein. I like to do this with a colt by bumping him in the elbow with the side of my stirrup, or by pressing my boot heel in the belly near the back cinch.

I can also slow this colt down to a walking turn-around, making him step all the way across his inside front foot with the outside foot, while I watch his feet over his inside shoulder. This will teach him that he can turn without interfering. I will do this slowly time and time again. I will not ask him to move any faster until he knows how to handle his front feet and has the confidence that he can turn without hurting himself.

Problem 2—Backs over his hocks. The solution is to add more forward motion to his turn-around, and one way is to trot a lot of circles, as explained under Problem 1. Some trainers also like to lope circles the same way...making them progressively smaller until the horse is turning in place.

Something else you can do with this horse is add impulsion on the outside. Go to his belly with your outside leg, and hold your inside rein. This will push him forward and make him drive to the bridle and step up. You can also make half or full turns, and drive him out of the turns with your outside leg.

Be careful not to put too much tension on the reins when turning him, as that will prevent him from moving freely—with forward motion.

Problem 3—Not on his pivot foot. That's easy for me to fix since I'm big on backing a colt. I would back him and make half-turns until he learns to handle his front end with his inside hind foot stationary, or isolated.

Problem 4—Lacks impulsion. When a colt is lazy or just not listening, he needs to be motivated to come around faster, and I'll usually swat him with my rein down the outside rear leg. You don't have to worry about losing the hindquarters when you do this, because any time you whack a horse on the rear end, his hind legs are going to come up under him. Plus as long as you whack him on the outside rear leg, you will keep him on his pivot foot. And it's going to motivate him to move, NOW!

If swatting the colt down the hind leg doesn't work, a knowledgeable rider could boot or spur the colt in the belly, or even in the shoulder. I say "knowledgeable" because he has to be savvy enough to know which method would be best for the particular colt. I personally like to leave the shoulder alone as much as possible because if you harass it too much, you sometimes lose the rear end—it will jump right out of the ground.

This is not to say I'll never poke a horse with a spur, because there are very few horses who never need to be spurred. There is a time and place for it, if you know how to use spurs correctly. Sometimes you need something a little sharper than a nudge of your heel to correct the horse when part of his body is out of position, or when he doesn't respond to your leg. Like when you are in the show ring and you need an instantaneous reaction. Once a horse is trained, it's okay to use an outside spur for impulsion because by this time he should have his form correct and he will stay on his pivot foot.

I wear my spurs most of the time while I'm riding. The few occasions I take them off are on horses that don't respond well to spurs...a light spur doesn't get the desired reaction, and a hard spur gets a radical reaction. With this kind of horse, it's often better to boot him hard in the belly with your heel. He will turn better, with less resistance, than he would with a spur.

If you don't know how to use spurs, you won't get the optimum out of your horse, and you will also have a tendency to poke him when you shouldn't. So it would be best to leave them off.

Whenever I do spur or spank a horse, I always follow this rule of thumb: Be sure when you add impulsion that you give direction with your rein. Otherwise the horse doesn't grasp the significance of why you are spurring, and you may get an undesired reaction.

For example, suppose I'm asking for more speed in a turn-around to the right. If I reach up and poke him in the left shoulder with my spur, I'll use my inside rein to direct that motion to the right. If I didn't, he might turn his head around and look to the left, for it's typical for a horse to look back to the side on which he's spurred.

There are also other situations you may encounter with your horse. Possibly he's dragging his outside shoulder, or his rib cage is hanging out. This is why it's so important that you are sitting with your seat screwed into the saddle: so you can feel what the horse is doing, and identify these situations.

If the outside shoulder is dragging, sometimes all that's necessary to correct this is a slight impulsion from the outside rein...or maybe a tap on the elbow with your stirrup.

If his rib cage is hanging out, his rear end may fishtail out from under him. The correction: drive the belly with your outside leg.

To make a fancy turn-around, you've got to have forward motion, you've got to have the horse on his pivot foot, and you've got to have the entire outside of his body moving. If the horse isn't giving the outside of his body, he can't continue to drive around his pivot foot. So if his ribs are out, or his shoulder, or his head, or even his hips, you're not going to get the full speed and flatness you want.

Speaking of the head, when the horse is turning, I want his head slightly to the inside so I can see his inside eye. This brings up another important reason why I always train colts in a snaffle. Because of the way the snaffle works, and the positioning of each ring on the side of the head, the snaffle brings the entire head and neck when the horse turns. A bosal—or any similar gear on the nose—pulls the chin but "leaves the ear"; that is, the head is tilted with the chin to the inside and the ear to the outside. You certainly don't want that.

One thing we haven't mentioned is clucking to the horse, as a form of impulsion in the turn-around. Many trainers do it, and so do I, but not to all of my horses. I definitely do not cluck to a horse that tends to be hyper, because it would only make him more hyper. I want to keep him quiet.

On the other hand, I will cluck to a slower horse, but he needs to relate the cluck to being poked in the belly, or smacked down the hindleg. Then when I cluck to him in the show ring, it means something.

A final note on turn-arounds. When I teach the colt to do a 360, and when he does it well and he feels comfortable doing it, I like to turn him a couple of times, say whoa, drop my reins, then just let him stand a few minutes. This enhances the relaxation of the horse, and lets him think about what he's done.

I also like to do this after a horse has made a good, long, hard stop. I'll let him stand so he can gather his wits, relax, and settle. It lets him know he did it correctly, and it's also a form of reward.

113

14 ROLL-BACKS

"Correct timing
by the rider helps
the horse perform
this maneuver cor-
rectly."

Fewer reining patterns call for roll-backs now as compared to years past, partly because many reining horse enthusiasts prefer sliding stops since they are more spectacular. Yet some patterns still require roll-backs, so we'll discuss them briefly.

By definition, a roll-back is a 180-degree turn over the hocks, executed just before the horse comes to a halt when making a stop. Immediately upon completing the turn, he moves out in the same tracks he made coming into the roll-back.

Our colt already has the foundation for a roll-back since he knows how to stop, back, and turn around. When I start him on roll-backs, I'll lope him down the arena, say whoa, and let him come to a complete stop. I back him up several steps, then make a 180-degree turn, and lope out of it. (To turn him, I'll primarily use a direct rein, some indirect rein, and a little bit of leg.)

I'll follow this procedure several times until the colt learns to turn and jump right out in a lope again.

When the colt's ready to make a finished roll-back, there's a little trick I use. In fact, I use it on almost all my horses to prevent them from turning around too far. I'll rein the horse through the first part of the roll-back (a 90-degree turn); then I release the rein pressure, but add my outside leg to complete the 180. This results in a smooth, flowing turn, with the horse moving out right in his tracks.

When you ask the horse to roll back, he's already moving since he hasn't completed his stop. Therefore reining him through the entire 180-degree turn puts too much momentum on him, and he

will turn too far. For example, if you are rolling back to the left, he will end up to the left of the tracks he made coming in.

I learned that if I rein the horse through the first 90 degrees, or quarter-turn, and then follow up with my outside leg, we end up right on our tracks.

When we come out of the roll-back, I don't want him to break and run wide open; I want full control. If I have done my homework out in the desert, I've taught this colt how to rate by speeding up and slowing down, time after time. Now when we come out of the roll-back, I should be able to pick up my hand and rate him at any speed I want. On occasion, I might want him to boil out of the roll-back, but I want him to wait for me to tell him.

If you have trouble getting your horse to roll-back correctly, analyze what he is doing. If he's not keeping his rear end planted, stop him straight, back a few steps, and roll him off. This teaches him where you want his rear end to be.

If he's dragging his outside shoulder, use a little more neck-rein, or bump him in the elbow with your stirrup. Or if he doesn't roll-back with any snap, swat him down the outside rear leg to add impulsion.

Correct timing on the rider's part also helps the horse perform this maneuver correctly. If the rider asks the horse to roll-back before he has slowed down enough in his stop, he will flounder around trying to do it.

1. Once a colt understands the fundamentals of a roll-back, I'll often work him alongside a fence, which will help contain him. I've asked this mare to stop, and I'm already using a little direct rein to roll her back before she comes to a complete stop. She has her hocks planted nicely.

2. She has picked up her pivot foot to reposition it as she rolls back on the fence, with very little effort on my part.

I've trotted this young mare down the fence and asked her to roll- back to the left. She's coming back very pre- cisely on a light rein.

1. A sequence of three photos showing the palomino mare rolling back to her left. Here, she's moving along the fence at a collected lope, slightly angled toward the fence.

2. *I ask her to stop, and then use a combination of indirect and direct rein to ask her to turn. My outside leg is ready to apply impulsion if necessary.*

3. *Her hocks are positioned correctly and she comes around with a lot of snap.*

15 ADVANCING TO THE BRIDLE

"The best reining horses I've ever ridden have been in the hackamore for a full year prior to the bridle."

The ideal in training a bridle horse is to take him from the snaffle into the hackamore, and from the hackamore into the bridle. You can skip the hackamore, but if I have my choice, I'll go to the hackamore after the snaffle. I feel that the longer you keep a horse in the hackamore, the better. The best reining horses I've ever ridden have been in the hackamore for a full year prior to the bridle. I developed their skills in the hackamore equally as well as I did in the snaffle, putting a good, solid foundation on them.

By hackamore, of course, I'm not talking about a mechanical hackamore that has shanks and a curb chain, and works on leverage. That type does have an occasional place in a training program to correct a particular problem, or for riding a finished horse, such as for trail riding or in timed events. But it has no role in a good training program for the reined horse.

When our colt is ready, I'll ride him in the snaffle and hackamore simultaneously for several weeks; I'll put a snaffle bridle on him, and the hackamore under it. Since the horse is under good control in the snaffle, I use it to ease him into the hackamore so I don't have to rough him up with the hackamore (bosal).

I'm very careful when I ride a colt in the hackamore, and I like to use a little heavier, looser-fitting bosal. The added weight gives it more feel to the colt, helping him learn how to respond to it. The looser fit makes it drop off the chin readily when I release the pressure, again helping the colt learn how to work in it. If it didn't drop off, he wouldn't learn the give and take.

Once the colt knows how to respond correctly, I find a bosal that he's comfortable in, and works the best in. Some horses like a bosal that fits snugly around the nose; others like a looser fit. Horses that are sensitive will get along better in a softer, lighter bosal of braided latigo, rather than a heavier bosal of braided rawhide.

On the majority of my horses, I use a little looser kind of bosal so that when I take hold of it, it works more on the nose than on the chin. This is necessary for the proper response. Yet I'm very careful not to rough up the nose because it's so important. Without a good nose, you won't have a good hackamore horse. Sometimes I'll even wrap the nose of the bosal with a material like Sealtex to keep the nose soft.

I don't worry that much about the chin. You can rough up the chin and still have a good nose, and sometimes I'll work on the chin a little more than on the nose. If you work on the chin, usually the horse's head will stay in a more natural position, or even be up a little bit. When you work on the nose, he'll usually drop his head down into the hackamore a little more. You have to do both to keep proper control of the horse.

When I'm riding the colt with both a snaffle and hackamore, I'll hold the left reins in my left hand, and the right reins in my right. I'll use the hackamore and snaffle reins simultaneously until the

118

When a colt is ready
to move into the
hackamore, I'll ride
him in both a snaffle
and a hackamore for a
few weeks.

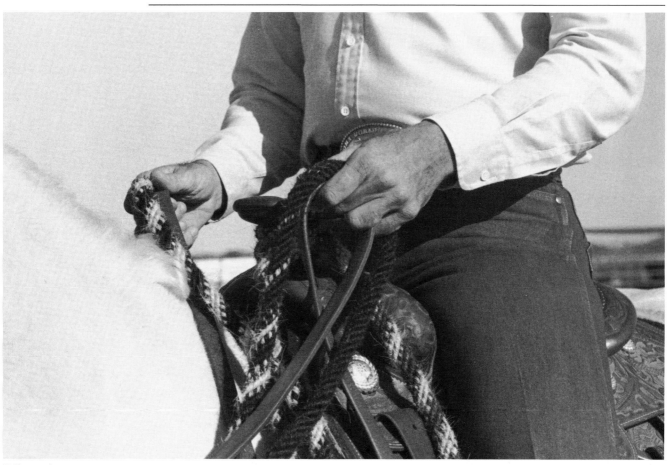

When a horse is in both the hackamore and snaffle, I'll hold both left reins in my left hand, and right reins in my right hand. This simultaneous pull gradually teaches the horse how to respond correctly to the hackamore.

horse finally relates to the hackamore as well as he does the snaffle. Then I'll stop using the snaffle, and ride with just the hackamore, schooling the horse in all the maneuvers he's already learned until he does them equally well in the hackamore.

There are precautions to take. When you turn the horse in a hackamore, you are pulling on the lower part of his jaw rather than his mouth. But you still want his entire head, ears, neck, and body to follow, just like you do in the snaffle. Make sure the "whole horse" is coming when you pull on the hackamore so you get the same correct movement as you do in the snaffle.

Also remember that a hackamore is not made to tug on. If you take a straight pull, often the horse can jam his nose right through the hackamore and maybe get away from you. You'll get much better results out of the hackamore by using a give-and-take motion with your hand. Then the horse will have less tendency to take hold of the hackamore and bull through it.

But regardless of what you use on the horse—snaffle, hackamore, curb bit—if

I like a little heavier, looser-fitting bosal on a colt. The looser fit makes it drop off the chin readily when I release the pressure.

120

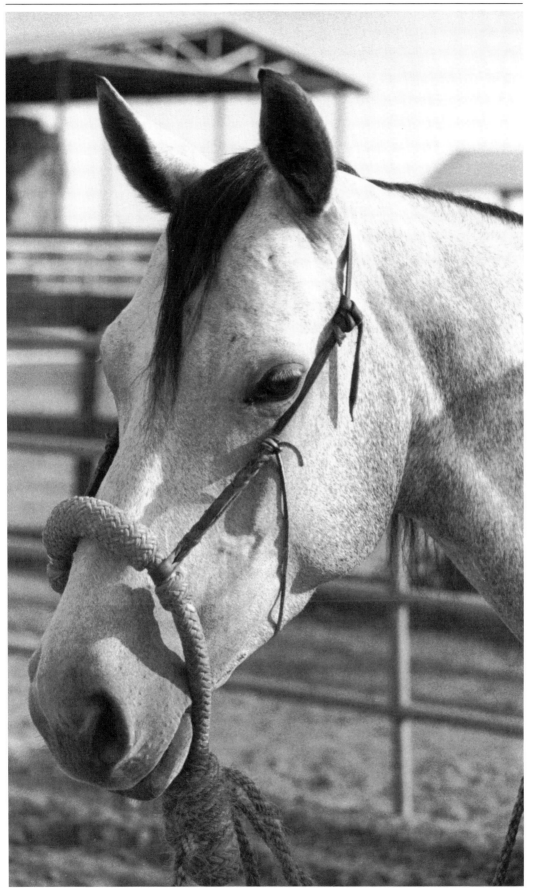

This shows where I like the bosal to be positioned on the nose. Note the thin piece of leather I use as a hanger, and the thong under the jaw to keep the hanger from getting into the eyes.

121

Once the colt graduates to just the hackamore, I school him in all the maneuvers he's learned in the snaffle. In asking this gray mare to turn around, I'm using a direct rein for direction and an indirect rein for impulsion.

you abuse him with it to the point he gets mad, he can take his head away from you. The horse has incredible strength in his head and neck and there's no way you can out-muscle him.

We have to use common sense and know that whenever we do take hold of the horse, we should have the advantage. In other words, you should have him pointed in a certain direction so that if he gets confused, or tries to take his head away from you, he will go where you have him pointed—such as in a circle where it's easier to regain control.

As I mentioned earlier, I like to keep a horse in the hackamore at least one full year. Then I move him into what we call two reins—using a light bridle and the hackamore simultaneously, I'll usually use a small, pencil-type bosal under the bridle.

The kind of bit I use depends on how I feel about the horse. Is he heavy-headed, or light? But generally I use a bit that's fairly thick in the bars of the mouthpiece because the horse can feel this bit better and take a little more hold, and because

it's a lot milder than a bit with thin bars. I use a leather chin strap.

I want to give this horse every chance to be light in the bridle. Some horses that are heavy in the snaffle turn out to be exceptionally light with a curb bit. Therefore if a horse was heavy in the snaffle, I don't automatically put him in a severe bit to begin with. Then I have nowhere to go later.

As a horse develops over the years, I want to advance him into a little more sophisticated kind of bit so he'll stay light. I don't want to advance him so quickly I don't have anything left to go to. It's like saying, "My horse is heavy in the snaffle so I'm going to put a thin, twisted-wire snaffle on him, tie his mouth shut, and rough up his mouth to get him light." It would be better to take your time and allow this horse to find out by himself how to be light. You do this by using your hands in the proper manner…keeping them light, and after you reprimand the horse, becoming light again. This works much better than trapping a horse in a situation where, be-

122

cause of soreness, he becomes light temporarily, because just surely as the sun always rises in the east, he'll get heavy again.

You have to look at training as a long-range project. If you approach it from the standpoint that "I've got to make him do this by tomorrow," he won't last very long.

I sort of got off the track here, so let's go back to putting the horse in the hackamore and bridle. When I'm riding in the two reins, as it's called (even though there are four reins), I hold the bridle reins differently. Let's assume I plan to work the horse on some maneuvers to the right. I'll put both bridle reins in my left hand, along with the left hackamore rein, and hold the right hackamore rein in my right hand.

As I ask the horse to circle or turn, I can use an indirect rein on the left side of his neck, and help him by giving a direct pull on the right hackamore rein.

When I plan to turn the horse to the left, I'll change hands, putting the bridle reins and right hackamore rein in my right hand, and left hackamore rein in my left hand.

This helps the horse learn to neck-rein, and to maintain the basic correct position when I ask him to turn around. The first thing I want him to do in a turn-around is get on his hocks. Second is to start turning his head and neck. Then I want him to move his front end, stay on his hocks, and turn. By holding the reins in this manner, I can help him turn correctly without his becoming frustrated or confused, as he would if I were sud-

"You have to look at training as a long-range project."

When the horse is in the two reins and I'm working him to the right, I'll put both bridle reins and the left hackamore rein in my left hand, and hold the right hackamore rein in my right hand.

When a horse is still in the two reins, but almost ready to go straight up in the bridle, this is how I ride him one-handed. My right hand is holding the romal.

*Same hand position
viewed from the left.*

denly using just one hand instead of two.

I'll ride him in the two reins until I no longer have to use the hackamore reins to help him stop, turn, or do anything else. This takes a lot of time, and I don't want to dwell on it here. Just go slowly and easily. I don't ever rush a horse in the bridle. I take my time, and do everything methodically so I don't confuse him now that he's in the bridle, because I'm going to set his foundation in the bridle for the rest of his life.

Skipping the Hackamore

A lot of people go right from the snaffle to the bridle, and that's all right. I've darn sure done it myself with quite a few horses. I will only say that if you go right to the bridle, you should ride with two hands and give the horse direction. And you should do this for a much longer period of time than if you had taken him through the hackamore stage. You should always be aware of what the horse is doing with his head, because it's so easy for it to get out of position, especially if you go to neck-reining too soon.

I'd also like to mention that I frequently put a horse back in the snaffle for schooling. I put his foundation on him with the snaffle, and the foundation is something to build on as well as something to go back to.

125

16 RUNNING A PATTERN

Step by step through AQHA Pattern No. 3

Among the reining patterns being used today, AQHA's No. 3 is one of my favorites because it allows a horse to demonstrate so many things with a lot of speed and pizzazz. No. 5 is also a favorite for the same reasons, but let's assume the judge has asked for No. 3.

One reason I like this pattern is because the first thing you do is run and stop. If you make a fast, pretty run and get a spectacular stop with distance in your slide, that immediately shows the brilliance of your horse and will impress the judge and your peers.

Before making your first run, however, study the footing in the arena. Know approximately where the best or most suitable ground is before making your run. Check for dips and holes, such as where the third barrel was set up in a barrel pattern. When making your stops, avoid ground that is uneven, sticky, wet, or where several horses have already stopped and dug it up. The best footing is dry, flat, smooth, and consistent.

Do this before starting the pattern because you should not be looking at the ground while you are running, or at the spot where you want to stop. If you do, your body will anticipate the stop—even though you may not be aware of it. The horse will pick up those subtle signals emitting from your body, and he may begin anticipating the stop.

Stopping a reining horse is like riding a jumping horse; you never look at the fence immediately in front of you—you look at the next fence. On a reining horse, look at the arena fence, or even a point beyond that when you are making a run-down the full length of the arena.

This will help keep the horse from anticipating, and will also keep you relaxed so you don't tighten up. When I am ready to stop, I concentrate to make sure I release my hand a little bit to give the horse a minute amount of slack in the reins before I say whoa and sit down. Next, I pick up the reins, but only to the point where the pressure starts the horse into the ground; then I let him pull me on through the stop.

When I say "let him pull me," I don't mean he's tugging my arm off, or rooting his nose out. I simply want to emphasize that I am not over-pulling him, which is easy to do in the show ring when you are so anxious to have him stop well. I pull just enough to get the kind of stop I want. If you don't over-pull, the horse will stay more relaxed in his mouth, head, neck, shoulders, and front legs— and you'll get one of those pretty stops when the horse slides behind and stays mobile in front.

After you stop, the pattern says you should back immediately. But I'm going to move my hand forward very slightly to release the pressure; i.e., release the chin strap and give the mouth some relief before taking a fresh hold for the backup. Releasing the pressure, even for a few seconds, gives the horse time to collect his thoughts and be ready to do whatever I next ask. And giving the mouth momentary relief might also help him keep it closed when I ask him to back.

To back, I take hold of the reins only

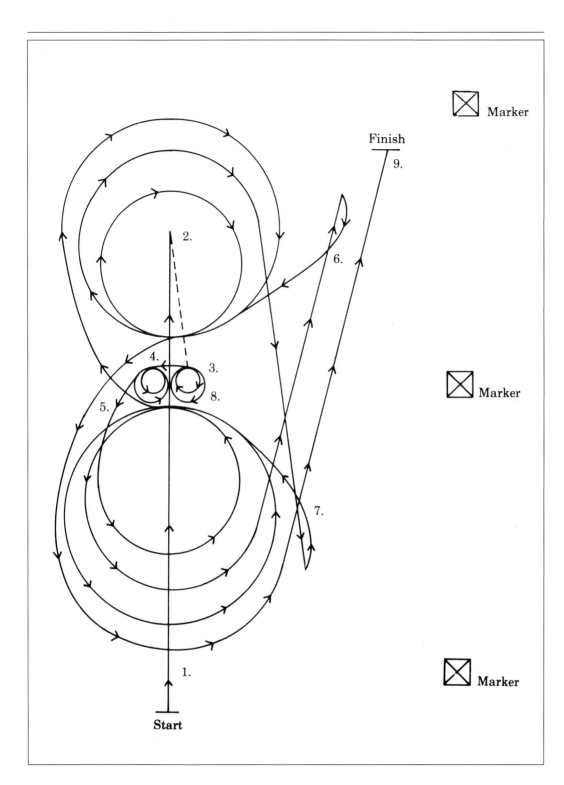

Finish

Marker

Marker

Marker

Start

AQHA Pattern Number 3
(Courtesy American Quarter Horse Association)

1. Run past center of arena and do a sliding stop.

2. Back immediately to center of arena—hesitate.

3. Do 2 spins to the right.

4. Do 2 1/4 spins to the left—hesitate.

5. Beginning on left lead, make a small slow circle, then begin a large fast circle. Do not close this circle, but run straight down the side past center marker and do a right roll-back, (at least 20 ft. from fence or wall).

6. Continue back to center of arena, horse should be on right lead at canter. Make a small slow circle to the right, then begin a large fast circle. Do not close this circle, but run straight down the side past center and do a left roll-back (at least 20 ft. from fence or wall).

7. Continue back to center of arena, horse should be on the left lead at canter.

8. Make a large fast circle to the left at center of arena. Change leads and make a large fast circle to the right, at center of arena. Change leads and begin a large, fast circle to the left. Do not close this circle, but run straight down the side past the center marker and do a sliding stop (at least 20 ft. from fence or wall).

9. Walk to judge and stop for inspection until dismissed.

10. The bridle may be dropped at the judge's discretion.

127

Loping a small circle with light contact.

enough so he backs with the dispatch I want. Over-pulling detracts from the smoothness, and might also make the mouth open and the head go up. To keep him backing straight, I use my legs, and the rein on each side of his neck.

You should back to the center of the arena, opposite the middle marker. Now the pattern asks for two spins to the right. But before I start, I let my horse rock forward just a little bit so he's not so deep on his hocks. When a horse is really low on his hocks, he can't turn around as quickly and fluidly as when he's standing up a bit more.

True, we trained this horse to turn around on his hocks. But if he's locked down in the ground from backing up, or if he's in heavy ground, it's wise to let him rock forward just one step so his center of gravity shifts forward a little bit. He'll still be on his hocks, and when I pick up the reins to turn him, he'll plant his pivot foot and turn.

When turning the horse around, it's important that you maintain your rhythm with that of the horse; you have to stay right in sync with him so you don't upset his rhythm. To keep him turning smoothly, I keep the outside rein on his neck, with just the right amount of pressure on it so he doesn't rock back too far, or move too far forward. I apply impulsion by clucking, or by hustling him with my outside leg or foot.

Just before he completes the second turn, I say whoa, and drop the pressure off his neck. In the split second it takes for me to do this and for him to react, we have completed two full turns.

Before asking him to make the 2 1/4 turns the other way, I hesitate a moment to allow him to think, and reposition himself. My reins are semi-loose. Then I pick the reins up, touch him on the neck with the outside (right) rein, and apply impulsion, and he begins turning to the left. This time, I let him complete two full turns before I say whoa and take the pressure off his neck. In the time it takes for him to react and stop, he's completed the final 1/4 turn. You can't expect to burn a horse through 2 1/4 turns and then ask him to stop dead on cue; it won't happen, and he'll end up making 2 1/2 turns and be facing the wrong way.

Before starting the circles, I let my horse relax for a few seconds, and show the judge and the crowd that he can settle after running and spinning.

When I start the left circle, I want my horse to break into the left lead immediately...no walking or trotting. I pick up the reins to gather the horse together, make sure his body is straight, and apply my right leg.

The first circle should be small and slow, and I am careful to stay well within the end marker—so I have space to make a larger circle without going beyond the marker. This circle should be a nice, easy lope on light contact, and when I come back to the center again, I should be at the same spot where we started—facing the middle marker.

At this point, the horse might be thinking "change leads and circle to the right." But we have to continue to the

128

"I know the horse well enough, and he knows me well enough, that he just feels when I want him to move on faster."

Galloping a larger, faster circle, collected and alert, and ready to do whatever I might ask.

left, and make a bigger and faster circle. Therefore I keep very light outside rein pressure on his neck, and continue loping at the same speed across the middle of the arena. If I were to speed up now, the horse might misjudge my cue and jump into his right lead.

After several strides across the middle, the horse realizes we are continuing to the left, and I ease him into a hand gallop. To build speed, I don't drive the horse with my outside leg, or use any other cue. Instead, he automatically accelerates as I relax the rein pressure on his neck to let him move into a larger circle. A lot of this is also the communication between the horse and me. I know him well enough, and he knows me well enough, that he just feels when I want him to move on faster. This way, our transition from slow to fast is very smooth.

When we come to the top of this circle, I begin straightening the horse for the run-down and the stop. I have to be careful because the horse thinks he's supposed to close up the circle.

I straighten him out by evening the rein pressure and putting my right leg on him. Yes, it sounds more logical to use my left leg, but it isn't. Remember, the horse is arcing to the left. When I use the reins to straighten his front end, I use my right leg to straighten his body and to prevent him from moving off to the right. In other words, I have him in a "vise" between my hand and leg.

When he is straight, I gradually let him build speed so he is really driving and elevated when I ask him to stop. Again, I know where I want him to stop, and I look beyond that area. But I know when we reach it, and then I release him momentarily before saying whoa, sitting down, and pulling back.

Since the pattern calls for a roll-back instead of a full stop, I don't complete the stop. Just as the horse reaches the end of his momentum, I roll him over his hocks to the right without letting him settle, and head back to the center point of the arena. I am cruising right along, but not as fast as I went into the stop and roll-back because my first circle to the right is supposed to be slow and small. As we approach the center of the arena, I slow him even more—into a nice, easy lope.

I make each of the circles to the right the same size as I did the left-hand circles, and follow the same procedure when I move the horse from the small circle into the larger, faster one. When we reach the top of the large circle, I straighten him up (using my reins and left leg) and let him gather speed for the run-down.

This time we roll-back to the left, return to the center of the arena, and go immediately into a large fast circle to the left, change leads, make a large fast circle to the right, change leads, and go into another large fast circle to the left. But instead of closing this circle, we gallop down the arena and stop...a full, sliding stop this time. I let the horse settle for a few seconds, then walk to the judge so he can inspect the bridle if he wishes.

17 PSYCHOLOGY OF TRAINING

"You tailor your training program to fit each horse."

To people who have not been around horses, a horse is a horse. To them, horses all look basically alike, they all eat hay and oats, and they all act pretty much the same. But as horsemen know, every horse is an individual. Each one has his own personality, temperament, quirks, likes and dislikes, sensitivity (or lack of), and level of intelligence.

Never is this knowledge of how horses differ more important than in training, because what works on ol' Bay might backfire on ol' Sorrely. This doesn't mean that you get away from your basic fundamentals, but that you tailor your training program to fit each horse. It's like looking at a road map that shows several different routes to your destination; you pick the one that best suits you. In training, you pick the route that best fits each horse.

Because horses are individuals, they vary in how much work they need. Some need to be ridden six or seven days a week; others get along better on four, and just about every horse benefits from an occasional vacation.

I ride my horses an average of four days a week, and when I'm out of town, they are generally turned out every day for free exercise, or ridden by one of my assistants out in the desert to keep them legged up. They don't get any schooling, just riding. Often when I return and get back on a particular horse, I'm surprised at how well he is doing—he may be better than he ever was.

Sometimes he actually *is* better, after having a vacation—he has had time to absorb his training. But sometimes it's just that I can see him in a better perspec-

Relaxing for a few minutes in the desert.

tive. It's like watching a youngster grow. When I see our little girl every day, she doesn't seem to be growing at all. But after I've been away for a couple of weeks and return home, it seems as if she's shot up three inches.

Although I ride my horses four days a week, I'm not training on them all the time, especially a reining horse. You have to let a reining horse relax and gather his thoughts. That's when I ride him out in the desert. I loosen up the reins, let him drop his head, and do a lot of quiet walking, jogging, and loping.

I can't emphasize enough how important this is…getting the horse away from

the barn and arena, and letting him relax and look around. It keeps him fresh, and greatly helps to prevent problems from developing. Problems like tail switching or tail wringing, anticipating lead changes, scotching on run-downs, and a generally unhappy appearance. Drilling a horse continually on any event or maneuver will soon destroy his enthusiasm for it, and lead to bad habits.

Even when I am working a horse in the arena, I do not work him on all parts of the reining pattern every time I ride him. One day, for example, I might work him on stops. I'll gallop around the arena, or diagonally across it, and stop at various places. Rarely do I gallop him down the middle because that teaches him to always expect to stop about 30 feet from the fence. I'll gallop around the arena, or diagonally across it, so he never knows when or where I might ask him to stop.

On the next day, maybe I'll lope circles, working on correct positioning. The third day, I might work on turn-arounds. And on the fourth day, I might work on some trail course obstacles, or

let him follow some cows around in the cutting pen—just to do something different with him to keep his mind fresh, even though he may never make a trail horse or cutting horse.

The fifth day, I might ride him out on the desert, on a loose rein, and let him totally relax while we jog and lope. On his days off, he is turned out for further relaxation. A horse doesn't need to be ridden every day to progress. In fact, some horses improve faster when ridden only every other day.

One thing I never do at home is work a horse on patterns. I school him on various parts of the pattern, as just mentioned, and once he knows all of them, it's easy to put them together in the show ring. This helps prevent the horse from anticipating what's next when actually running a pattern.

Occasionally I'm asked how I would start an older horse on reining, such as a horse that's only been pleasured. A lot depends on his age, how set he is in his ways, and how well he has been trained. But generally, I'd start him as if he were a

Even if a reining horse has no future as a cutting horse, I'll often work him on cattle to give him something else to think about. This helps keep him fresh.

131

Expensive Hobby in a figure-eight, with his ears up and looking content.

colt. I'd put him in a snaffle bit, see if he understands leg pressure, make sure he's got a good back-up and a 180-degree turn, and make sure his mouth is right before going on to fancy things.

Just because he's broke doesn't mean you can knock on him to turn around, or haul on him to get him to stop. You've got to go back to the basics and make him understand these new things. However, he can probably advance much faster than a colt if he's already been in the bridle, is well-broke, and—most important—has no serious problems.

When you are training, there is no place for anger. Every good trainer knows that, and it's easy to say it, but usually we all have to learn the hard way how true it is. Obviously if a horse reaches around and bites your foot, that's darn sure a time to reprimand him. But discipline him in a manner he understands, then quit. Don't keep on. That will only make him fear you instead of respecting you, and might also make him rebellious.

When you get on a horse, don't have vengeance in your heart. If you are upset because your wife's mad at you, or the mortgage payment is overdue, lock those emotions up. If you take your anger out on the horse, you might set his training back several weeks.

Don't forget that horses have feelings, too. If they could talk, I believe they'd tell us a few things about themselves that would help us in training them. We have to realize that they occasionally get up on the wrong side of the bed just like we do, and that they probably have some of the same ailments we do: headaches, sore muscles, aching joints. They can't tell us about them. That's why a rider must be sensitive to how his horse feels, and realize that on a bad day, the horse can't possibly give his maximum. We cannot expect 100% every time we ride our horses.

Suppose a horse isn't doing something quite right, like turning around. You school him and feel that you've done your best to get the point across to him, but he's still not right. Rather than get in a storm with him, it would be better to put him up and let him rest. When you get on him the next day, he might do it

132

just fine. Maybe he absorbed the lesson during the night, or maybe his headache or whatever is gone.

Sometimes when I'm having a problem with a horse, I'll get off in the arena, dally the reins around the horn, and let him wander around loose while I ride another horse. I'll think about the problem, what's causing it, and what I should be doing to correct it. When I get back on the horse, he's not hot, he's not mad, and I can begin to work out the sequence of correction. If I'd gone ahead with the horse and gotten in a storm with him, the only thing that would come out of it would be an intimidated horse.

By staying calm and cool, and keeping your wits about you, you can achieve optimum results from your correction. You can't if you get mad and go to thrashing. You must also realize exactly what to do to correct a horse to achieve the result you want.

There are many analogies between humans and horses, and training a young horse is just like training a child. You reprimand them when they are wrong, and praise them when they are right. And praise should be more than just absence of punishment.

To praise a horse, I like to drop the reins, let him stand, and pat him on the neck. To correct him, I can use my hands, legs, or the ends of the reins, whichever is appropriate.

There are also indirect ways you can reward a horse, like taking good care of him, which, of course, should be stand-ard procedure. Feeding him properly, keeping him well groomed, and turning him out so he can run and play…those things not only keep him feeling good, but are a reward, too. They make him feel wanted, and appreciated, and he'll respond to that, just like a person would. On the other hand, to be isolated in a stall or pen and ignored is an effective means of punishment to some horses …especially those that enjoy being around people, and being ridden and used.

Working Expensive Hobby on cattle was a big reason why he stayed fresh for so many years. In addition to showing him in cowhorse classes, I also showed him in cutting the last two years before his retirement.

To praise a horse, I'll drop the reins, let him stand, and pat him on the neck.

18 PSYCHOLOGY OF SHOWING

Hot Chocolate Chex, owned by Marilyn Harris of Phoenix when I was showing him (late '70s), won all-around performance saddles at the Sun Country and Land of Enchantment circuits. **Louise Serpa Photo**

After all these months we finally have this horse trained and ready to show. But before taking the plunge, I like to trailer him to other arenas, and to horse shows where I'll just ride him around the grounds. This lets him get acquainted with different sights and sounds in a relaxed atmosphere—meaning I'm not putting any pressure on him like there'll be when I show him. I might even drop him in a pleasure class or two just for some actual experience in the show ring.

This will also tell me how he's going to act in an atmosphere that differs from his home environment. Does he get nervous and uptight? Or does he stay calm and take everything in stride? A horse that gets hyper may take more riding before his class to help him settle, whereas others need to be ridden just enough to loosen their muscles.

A lot of riders beat themselves in a reining class by over-schooling before the class. This is called "leaving the work outside," or "leaving the work in the practice ring," and it will take the brilliance off your work. In warming the horse up, use wise judgment and loosen him up just enough to prepare him to show to the peak of his ability.

Always remember the fundamentals: the position you want the horse to be in when you turn him around, and how you want him to stop. Don't get excited and forget how you do things, like saying whoa and sitting down before taking hold of his head when asking him to stop.

In actually running a pattern, stay

calm. Don't let your adrenalin pump you up so much that you put more pressure on the horse than he can handle—to the point that he doesn't even perform as well as he can at home. Only show the horse to his capability; do not push him to try and beat a horse that perhaps has more talent or experience. In doing that, you might blow your whole run and not even place. And you might create problems in the horse that will hinder him later on when he is ready for a pressure run.

It is important to remember that win, lose, or draw, there will always be another horse show, and there will always be another horse. Try and make this horse work the best that he possibly can at his present stage of training, and be satisfied that you have done that kind of job.

Although I like to win as much as anybody, I am more interested in showing off my workmanship—how I've trained and prepared this horse—and his ability, than I am in the placings. That's why I never try to beat somebody else. I simply show my horse to his maximum capability. I don't go into a class with the thought, *I am going to win,* and pressure my horse beyond his ability, or readiness. But if he has been prepared, seasoned, and has the talent, I darn sure ride him to his maximum capability.

When watching a reining run, the judge is looking at the overall picture, so know how your horse looks the prettiest and smoothest. In my opinion, position and control are far more important than speed. It's better to travel at a moderate speed and have good form than it is to highball through the pattern with rough circles and bad stops. If a horse can handle a lot of speed and still maintain form, great! But if not, throttle him down a few notches and keep his form correct. Also remember his strong points and try to capitalize on them, and smooth over his weaker points the best you can.

If he's a good, hard stopper, razzle-dazzle the judge and crowds with your stops. If he's not flashy in his turn-arounds, go easy and try to keep his form correct.

You have to be thinking all the time, not only how to best show the horse, but also to stay on pattern. That's not always easy, and even the best of riders oc-casionally go off pattern. If it happens to you, don't let it eat at you; there's always another show.

A lot of success in showing depends on your not getting nervous, and keeping your wits about you. Don't let the runs that precede you bother you. Sometimes it's better not to watch them. And don't let the performances of other horses in the warm-up pen dictate how you're going to show your horse. Always show your horse in the style or fashion that fits him best. Don't try to show him according to the way others are showing their horses.

Maybe some of the other horses can handle more speed than your horse. Or maybe some of them can burn the turn-arounds faster than your horse. On the other hand, maybe your horse can run a more precise pattern, with prettier circles and changes.

I'll guarantee that if you keep your cool and make a nice, correct run, your turn to win will come over a rider who runs hard, but makes a lot of mistakes. He might score higher than you today, but if you concentrate on building a foundation and correct positioning on your horse, you'll end up winning when your horse is ready.

I don't mean to imply that you should always run an easy-going pattern. When your horse is ready, show him to win!

"A lot of riders beat themselves in a reining class."

Expensive Pony, reserve champion hackamore horse at the 1981 Phoenix A to Z Show, his first time shown. Becky and I raised this horse (by Hobby Horse and out of Pink Pony), and later sold him.
Jack Schatzberg Photo

135

19 PROFILE: AL DUNNING

Al Dunning leans back in his chair, his feet propped on the desk and the telephone to his ear. It is mid-afternoon, and he has been working horses since early morning. All day the phone in the barn office has rung constantly, and the messages have piled up.

While his assistants saddle the final set of horses, Al grabs a few minutes to answer several calls. Sometimes he wishes that the telephone had never been invented, but in today's equine industry, he knows that it cannot be ignored.

When he steps off his last horse of the day, he grabs the remaining messages and his briefcase, which serves as a traveling file cabinet, and drives quickly to the house in his golf cart. The Dunnings' attractive, Southwest-style home lies just a few hundred feet away.

His wife Becky is preparing supper for their daughter McKenzie before the baby sitter arrives. Later, Al and Becky are going to dinner with out-of-town guests, a frequent occurrence at the Dunning residence.

Many visitors are fellow trainers, or aspiring trainers. Sometimes they are looking for good horses to buy, but often they just want to spend several days riding, trying to absorb a few techniques from this tall young man, an acknowledged artisan in the training of horses.

To those genuinely interested in learning, Al is generous with both his time and advice, a reflection of the help he has received over the years, and of his philosophy that "we are put on this earth for a reason, and it is to share with others the knowledge the Lord has given us."

There have been three horsemen—Jim Paul, John Hoyt, and Don Dodge—who have been influential in Al's life, and from whom he has gained much of his knowledge. Al met Jim a few years after the Dunning family moved from the Chicago suburb of Wilmette to Scottsdale when Al was nine years old.

The youngest of four children, and the only boy, Al learned to ride in a flat saddle on bridle trails in Chicago-area parks and forests. "Even took a few jumps," he smiles. "Actually, it was my three sisters who were crazy about horses at that time—I just went along with them."

As a young boy, Al suffered from rheumatic fever and a heart murmur. "Although we moved to Arizona because we wanted to, it turned out to be good for my health."

The family soon purchased a mare named Roxie and kept her at a boarding stable. "She was the first of 27 horses we had between the time I was 12 and 19," Al recalls. "We did everything with her—barrel racing, games, riding her to friends' homes—all the things kids like to do with horses.

"I got into roping and riding calves, and began going to a few horse shows. I was having a ball, and it was a great time in my life. Especially when I went to a horse show and won a horsemanship class. Then I really got hooked. I began going to more shows, and as my sisters got older and began losing interest in horses, I inherited their horses."

Al was about 14 when he met Jim Paul. "I had never been around anyone quite like him, and to best describe him, I'd say he was darn sure what a young man would consider the John Wayne-type. He became a father image to me."

Don Dodge.

Al rode with Jim from 1962 until 1969 and won a truckload of year-end high-point awards in the Arizona Quarter Horse Breeders Association and the Arizona Horse Exhibitors Association, including stock seat equitation and junior stock horses three years in a row.

From Jim, Al acquired a wealth of knowledge about training and handling all kinds of horses. "At that time, we were riding a lot of what I considered rough stock. Today, the horses we get are well-bred and easy to work with. But back then, a lot of them were cold-blooded and tough to handle, and required unorthodox methods of training compared to what we use today. I learned a lot about breaking horses of that type.

"Jim is an artist who can paint, draw, build, invent, and play the guitar. He can do all kinds of things, and it reflects in his horse training...he is meticulous about how he wants his horses to work. He's played a great part in my life, and I think the world of him."

Al began riding with John Hoyt in 1969 while he was attending Phoenix Junior College—and trying to sort out in his mind if he wanted to be a full-time professional trainer. "John was like Jim in some respects, but didn't have to use as many different techniques. John more or less had his kit together, and from him I learned that you've got to have a training program you like, and one you can stick with in order for your training to have continuity and a sense of direction."

It was while riding with John Hoyt

Rosetta Chex winning the hackamore championship at the 1981 Phoenix A to Z Show. This mare is owned by Brett Stone of Scottsdale.
Jack Schatzberg Photo

Skipit Chex, owned by Pat Close of Colorado Springs, winning the hackamore class for mares at Del Mar, 1979.
Fallaw Photo

when Al made up his mind that he definitely wanted to be a professional trainer. "I was a junior at Arizona State University when I retired from my college career and hung out my shingle." This was in 1971, and Al quickly had 15 horses in his barn. "I was lucky because several trainers in the area were going out of business as I was getting started."

Success in the show ring also came quickly. "We did okay in 1971 and '72, and then in '73 we started doing *real* well," Al states, not immodestly, but matter-of-factly. Not until 1975 did he begin showing out of state, and in the

following eight years (through 1982), produced eight world champions. "We've had four champions at the World Championship Quarter Horse Show, three at the AJQHA Finals, and one at the Quarter Horse Congress in the NRHA open reining."

These championships were earned in reining, working cowhorse, and western riding—and in stock seat equitation and reining at the AJQHA Finals by youth riders Al has coached.

Many high-caliber pleasure horses have also emerged from Al's barn, both western and bridle path hack. Although

138

Al does not ride flat saddles today, he has trained hunt-seat horses that his wife Becky and customer/owners have shown with considerable success, including two reserve champions at the World Show.

In addition to the shows already mentioned, Al has frequently competed at the Cow Palace (Grand National Horse Show) in San Francisco, the Santa Barbara National Horse Show, Del Mar in southern California, the Phoenix A to Z Show, Quarter Horse circuits in California, Nevada, New Mexico, and Colorado, and the CRCHA Snaffle Bit Futu-

rity in Reno. In only ten years of training professionally, he has proven himself capable in all kinds of competition. And he drives himself to maintain this winning edge.

"I feel you stop being successful when 1) you quit trying to learn 2) you quit trying to improve, or 3) you quit altogether. I'm darn sure not going to quit, I'm not going to stop trying to learn, and I'm darn sure trying to improve all the time."

Don Dodge became a winter resident on the Almosta Ranch several years ago when Al took a long, hard look at cut-

Ready Chex, AQHA Honor Roll high-point stallion in reining and reserve champion in senior reining at the World Show in 1980. He was owned by Mimi Bimson of Scottsdale when Al was showing him.
LeRoy Weathers Photo

139

Snickelfritz Chex, high-point reining horse on the 1982 West Coast and Arizona Sun Country circuits. He's owned by Tim and Barbara Dietz of Scottsdale.
LeRoy Weathers Photo

His talent and skills are legendary, and Dodge-trained cutting horses are noted for the solid foundation they have received. Under Don's tutelage, Al has already enjoyed modest success in cutting. This includes several high-points in Quarter Horse circuit competition, state champions, and an AQHA Superior Cutting Horse. He has also made the finals in cutting at the World Show in Oklahoma City.

In 1981, Al took a horse for the first time to the richest and most prestigious cutting of all, the NCHA Futurity in Fort Worth. Although he lost a cow in the first go-round, he didn't let disappointment gnaw at him. "When I show a horse, I feel the way an artist must feel when he has his paintings on display. He might not sell any of them, but if people appreciate his work, he feels satisfied. That's the way I feel when I have trained a horse and he works to the best of his ability, even though we might not win.

"In this particular case, the mare worked really well despite the fact we lost a cow...which really wasn't her fault. She reflected the training that I had put into her, a lot of people liked the way she worked, and I sold her for a bunch of money. There was no reason for me not to feel happy and satisfied. Besides, there's always another futurity."

Al's positive attitude also applies when he has gone off pattern in reining. "I'm good at that!" he grins. Take the Equus Show at Denver (1977) as an example. The open reining had two go-rounds and a finals, and had attracted many of the very best reiners from the West Coast, Midwest, and East. It was like the World Series of reining. Al was showing Expensive Hobby and their two runs were so brilliant that they were leading by 13 points going into the finals when, alas, they made one too many spins in a turn-around.

"But," says Al, "I derived more acclaim from that show than maybe any other I've been to. I was thrilled with my horse and thrilled with his performance, which gave me a tremendous amount of satisfaction in how well I had prepared him. I would have been even happier if we had won, of course, but I still felt like I had the world by the tail."

Al doesn't hesitate to give credit for his success and attitude to his strong be-

ting. "That was one event I hadn't done. I roped when I was a kid, did a little barrel racing, and have shown horses in all kinds of events—reining, cowhorse, pleasure, western riding, trail, halter, equitation—the whole Molly Ann. Cutting is different, and requires technical training and horsemanship that I didn't know much about." In other words, a new challenge.

"A long time ago, one of the greats told me, 'If you want to learn something, learn from a champion. Learn the methods that worked for him, benefit from his ideas, and avoid the mistakes he made.' It's like reading history books in school...not only do we learn from our heritage, but we learn which ideas worked or didn't work for countries and governments in the past. Well, I go along with that advice. I really believe that a young man in the training business needs to have guidance from someone who has been a champion and has great knowledge."

Don Dodge qualifies on both counts.

lief in the virtues of Christianity. He is not one who pushes his religious convictions onto others, but when asked, he talks about them freely.

He went to Sunday school and church regularly when he was growing up, but it was not until he was training horses that he became aware of the strength and values to be found through Christianity. "I was working hard and striving to be successful at what I was doing, and was forgetting that there are more important things in life than winning first place at a horse show.

"Since then, I've come to realize that the Christian life has helped me more than anything else. In fact, without the help I've received through Christian fellowship, I don't believe I'd be where I am today. I feel that if you make the effort at all times to be a good person, it will reflect in everything else you do—even training horses. I'm not saying I'm successful at it 100 percent of the time, but I do make a conscious effort to live by the good book."

From the kitchen, Becky calls McKenzie to come and eat. At this point in her young life, McKenzie isn't fussy about what her mom dishes up, and it's a good thing. "I hate to cook!" Becky laughs. "Fortunately, we're not real big on fancy meals around here, and we all like casseroles. One reason why I enjoy company so much is because we go out to eat."

An accomplished rider herself, Becky met Al through horse activities when she was in her mid-teens. She was taking riding lessons for a Girl Scout badge at the Arizona Stables where Al boarded a couple of horses, when someone introduced them. "We got to know each other better when we were showing at local non-approved shows," Becky remembers, "and we started dating in 1967 when I was 16."

Becky was taking lessons at this time from John Hoyt, and she proved to be a thoroughly capable student. In 1969 she and Al waged a friendly battle all year long for the youth all-around award in the Arizona Quarter Horse Breeders Association, and it was Becky who won the trophy saddle. "But it was close," she admits. "Between the two of us, we accumulated around 400 points, and I only

Al and Becky, competitors in the show ring before they were married.

won by about 7. We competed in barrels, poles, stakes, western pleasure, horsemanship, showmanship, reining, and western riding."

When Al and Becky announced their engagement (they were married in December 1971), her father, George Lasley, was not overly pleased, although he didn't make an issue of it. By that time,

141

"I think a horse trainer needs to be lucky...and I've been awfully lucky."

McKenzie is already learning how to ride horses with her dad.

Al had decided to become a professional horse trainer, and therein lay the reason for George's disappointment. Horse training in 1971 was not the lucrative profession it can be today. And, as Becky points out, "A lot of horse trainers didn't have a great track record when it came to family or financial stability. That's what bothered my dad, but he talked it over with both Al and me and made sure we understood his concerns." He also gave Al some fatherly advice, the gist of which Al still remembers:

"To be a success in the horse business, you have to lead a good, moral life. You cannot take so many horses that you cannot ride them all; you must give each horse a fair chance; you have to give customers their money's worth and treat them the way you'd like to be treated; and you must present yourself in the kind of manner that doesn't leave you open to criticism. If you do these things, and if you have any talent at all, you'll be a success."

George no longer worries about his daughter, because the Dunnings typify fulfillment of the American dream with their own home and training facilities, motor home, boat, and vacations in Hawaii. "After we were married," Becky says, "Al could have gone to work for someone else, but we decided to stay on

our own and start out on a small scale. It was a good decision, and now we have our own place."

The present Almosta Ranch got its start when Al and Becky bought ten acres of raw land "way out in the sticks in northeast Scottsdale," as Al puts it. They first built the main barn, then later their home—and most of their first neighbors were jackrabbits and coyotes. They have since bought two adjoining tracts, each with a house, and the entire parcel sits right in the path of the land developers' march into the desert. Because the Dunnings are well aware that the land is becoming too valuable for a training facility, they are starting to consider a new location in the Scottsdale area.

Investments like this have helped secure the Dunnings' future. "Al is very goal- and future-oriented," says Becky, "and he learned from his father as well as mine the value of investing money in something other than your own business. However," she adds with a laugh, "if he had to choose between buying stocks and bonds or a futurity prospect, he'd probably buy the futurity prospect."

Of course, a futurity horse can also be a solid investment, and more than a few of them have successfully graduated from Al's training program. Some he has bought; others he has raised, trained, and sold; and still others he has trained for customers. Whichever, a good futurity horse today can put money in the pocket of a trainer.

Relaxing between a steak dinner and dessert at one of the Dunnings' favorite eateries, Al talks about some of his good horses. "I think a horse trainer needs to be lucky," he muses, "and I've been awfully lucky. I was able to apprentice under some great hands, and I was lucky to get some darn good horses almost immediately. A great horse can give a horse trainer a name, and I got a tremendous horse shortly after I started training."

He's talking, of course, about Expensive Hobby, who carved a nationwide reputation for his prowess in hackamore, reining, and cowhorse classes, and who at the same time made Al known as a "great trainer." The acclaim is richly deserved. Hobby arrived in Al's barn as a green three-year-old, and it was Al who honed his skills and kept him at his peak for nine years. Nine l-o-n-g years when you consider the great number of reining flashes that are here this year and gone the next.

Expensive Hobby is a registered Quarter Horse gelding, owned by Georganna Stewart Shelley of Temecula, California. Georganna and her dad, Bud Stewart of Yuma, Ariz., were among Al's first customers when he began training, and they asked him to find a reining prospect for Georganna, who was then 17. Al had already seen a nice buckskin gelding being shown in California by Mehl Lawson. "Although the horse was still green, I could tell from the way he was built and the way he had been started that he would suit me and also make a good horse for Georganna," Al remembers.

Thus Expensive Hobby arrived in Al's barn in 1974. Al began showing him in the hackamore, winning 29 of 32 classes, including championships at the A to Z Show and Del Mar, and the reserve championship at the Cow Palace in 1975. The year 1976 launched Hobby's career in the bridle and, to briefly sum it up, he won the stock horse championships at the Phoenix A to Z Show (three times), Santa Barbara National, Del Mar (five times), and the NRHA open reining at the Quarter Horse Congress. At the World Championship Quarter Horse Show, Hobby won the senior reining once and the senior working cowhorse twice.

In May 1983, Expensive Hobby was formally retired, leaving quite a hole in Al's show string. However, the real proof of a trainer is whether he can make more than one great horse, and although there may never be another Expensive Hobby, Al has already produced a number of other winners. He's won the big shows with horses like Snickelfritz Chex, Ready Chex, Rosetta Chex, Skipit Chex, Hot Chocolate Chex, Cherizan, Pink Pony, Docs Cheshire Cat, Smokealot, and many more. Major wins are not necessarily limited to reining and cowhorses. He rode Mista Bull to the world championship in senior western riding at the 1976 World Show, and Bucket O Moonbeams in 1981. "The 1976 win was a pretty emotional one for me," he smiles. "Mista Bull was the first horse I'd

ever taken from scratch (unbroke) and gone all the way with."

There have been some mighty fancy pleasure horses schooled by this multi-talented trainer. Horses such as Miss Blue Moolah, The Mover, The Collateral, Misty Klondike, Mr. Strike It Rich, Diamonds Fame, Poco Don Dee, Big Johnny Star, Simple Dreams, Skipa Manana, Ultra Fashion, and Glowette, to name a few.

In the years to come, cutting and futurity horses will play a bigger role in Al's training program, because those are fast becoming the events to win. And undoubtedly his hard work and belief that "life gives back to a man what he puts into it" will help assure his future success.

—Pat Close

Smokealot, owned by Marilyn Harris of Phoenix, reserve champion hackamore horse at Del Mar, 1979.
Fallaw Photo

143

Western Horseman Magazine

Colorado Springs, Colorado

The Western Horseman, established in 1936, is the world's leading horse publication. For subscription information and to order other Western Horseman books, contact: Western Horseman, Box 7980, Colorado Springs, CO 80933-7980; 719-633-5524.

Books Published by Western Horseman Inc.

TEAM ROPING by Leo Camarillo
144 pages and 200 photographs covering every aspect of heading and heeling.

REINING by Al Dunning
144 pages and 200 photographs showing how to spin and slide.

CALF ROPING by Roy Cooper
144 pages and 280 photographs covering the how-to of roping and tying.

BARREL RACING by Sharon Camarillo
144 pages and 200 photographs. Tells how to train and compete successfully.

HORSEMAN'S SCRAPBOOK by Randy Steffen
144 pages and 250 illustrations. A collection of popular Handy Hints.

WESTERN HORSEMANSHIP by Richard Shrake
144 pages and 150 photographs. Complete guide to riding western horses.

HEALTH PROBLEMS by Robert M. Miller, D.V.M.
144 pages on management, illness and injuries, lameness, mares and foals, and more.

CUTTING by Leon Harrel
144 pages and 200 photographs. Complete how-to guide on this popular sport.

WESTERN TRAINING by Jack Brainard
With Peter Phinny. 136 pages. Stresses the foundation for western training.

BACON & BEANS by Stella Hughes
136 pages and 200-plus recipes for popular western chow.

STARTING COLTS by Mike Kevil
168 pages and 400 photographs. Step-by-step process in starting colts.

IMPRINT TRAINING by Robert M. Miller, D.V.M.
144 pages and 250 photographs. Learn how to "program" newborn foals.

TEAM PENNING by Phil Livingston
144 pages and 200 photographs. Tells how to compete in this popular family sport.

LEGENDS by Diane C. Simmons
168 pages and 214 photographs. Outstanding early-day Quarter Horse stallions and mares.

NATURAL HORSE-MAN-SHIP by Pat Parelli
224 pages and 275 photographs. Parelli's six keys to a natural horse-human relationship.